MEET YOUR NEIGHBORS

*New England
Portraits,
Painters, & Society,
1790-1850*

Essays by

Jack Larkin, Elizabeth Mankin Kornhauser, and David Jaffee

Catalog of the Exhibition by Jessica F. Nicoll

Caroline F. Sloat, editor

OLD STURBRIDGE VILLAGE,
STURBRIDGE, MASSACHUSETTS, 1992
DISTRIBUTED BY THE UNIVERSITY OF MASSACHUSETTS PRESS

"Meet Your Neighbors: New England Portraits, Painters, and Society, 1790-1850," Old Sturbridge Village, May 2, 1992-January 3, 1993

The exhibition, "Meet Your Neighbors: New England Portraits, Painters and Society, 1790-1850" was organized by Old Sturbridge Village. This catalog and the exhibition it accompanies were made possible, in part, through grants from the National Endowment for the Humanities, a federal agency.

CONTENTS

FOREWORD

OLD STURBRIDGE VILLAGE celebrates the opening of the *Meet Your Neighbors: New England Portraits, Painters, and Society, 1790-1850* exhibition as the entry into a new stage in the Museum's life cycle. This event brings to public view and scholarly attention a significant collection of non-academic portraits that has heretofore had little exposure through exhibition or publication. Further, *Meet Your Neighbors* demonstrates this museum's commitment to quality in collections, exhibitions, interpretation, and education.

The term neighbor has been used almost as long as people have settled near one another in a societal relationship. Old Sturbridge Village's depiction of the rural New England countryside of the 1830s identifies the interaction of neighbors as central to an understanding of community life. The houses and other buildings we have assembled here, from various parts of the region, were once home and work space to a remarkable group of individuals. In conjunction with this historic environment, *Meet Your Neighbors* offers a fascinating view of the people of a bygone era.

Crawford Lincoln,
President, Old Sturbridge Village

INTRODUCTION

PORTRAITS HAVE AN IMMEDIACY which makes them compelling windows on the past. As images, they provide tangible information about their subjects and the world in which they lived. As art and cultural artifacts they reveal the dynamic social, aesthetic, and economic forces that shaped them. *Meet Your Neighbors: New England Portraits, Painters, and Society, 1790-1850*, uses portraiture as a prism through which to look at rural New England society. In those years industrialization, immigration, and urbanization under-mined the old order and encouraged the emergence of a new class of Americans. This middle class redefined tastes and material standards in a wider cultural movement, creating a new age of abundance. *Meet Your Neighbors* focuses on artists, their patrons, and the community at large to shed light on these profound and complex social and economic changes.

From the perspective of the Museum, the exhibition has two primary goals. One is to increase the accessibility and usefulness of the portrait collection of Old Sturbridge Village through this public exhibition grounded in rigorous scholarship. The other is to display works from other collections that have not been extensively studied and exhibited. To this end, some thirty-nine portraits have been borrowed from public and private collections in the northeast for exhibition with forty-three likenesses (both large-scale and miniature) from this Museum's collection. This exhibition, and others like it, serve as a dynamic footnote to the recreated Village, complementing and expanding upon the visitor's experience within the richly detailed early-19th-century environment.

Meet Your Neighbors also explores the intricate networks of family, work, and commu-nity in early-19th-century New England. These themes are the focus of the Museum's interpretive and educational programs.

This unique exhibition and catalog would not have been possible without the support from the National Endowment for the Humanities. We continue to applaud and appreciate the contribution this funding agency makes to broaden the understanding of the humanities for all Americans. Our staff, however, have made this project happen and we thank this knowledgeable, talented, and skilled group of professionals. Special mention should be made of Jessica Nicoll, our Curator of Exhibits, and Project Director for *Meet Your Neighbors*. Finally, we are indebted to the lenders whose paintings contributed to the wholeness of this presentation.

Alberta Sebolt George,
Executive Vice President

NOTES AND ACKNOWLEDGEMENTS

THE EARLY-19TH-CENTURY PORTRAITS of *Meet Your Neighbors* reflect the burgeoning economy and optimism that buoyed residents of the new nation. Over the past three years of realizing this project, we have been similarly buoyed by our growing enthusiasm for our subject. At the start we faced the daunting challenge of pinpointing the artistic and historic meanings of these portraits. As we reviewed the current debates on the differentiation between non-academic and academic painting, or the concepts of plain and fancy, it became increasingly apparent that *Meet Your Neighbors* makes a contribution in that arena.

The paintings are fascinating, but are they art or craft? Study of the artists' lives reveals that most had a background in the "branches of painting," as understood in early-19th-century America. For them, making a living through art began with training in house-, sign-, chair-, and other decorative painting techniques. Many had to be content with an itinerant lifestyle, flexible enough to take commissions wherever there might be a demand.

Despite the apparent lack of formal training for artists, there was a highly sophisticated tradition of portraiture in rural New England by the second quarter of the 19th century. There were no academies in the United States at this time to provide instruction, but handbooks for artists were written by European academicians. Individuals who chose to forge a career in the arts also had access to the paintings of their peers, and to instruction from those who had benefited from European training. Decorative painters developed a style of portraiture characterized by the use of primary colors, limited shading, and pronounced two-dimensionality. A commercial impulse inspired the adaptation of decorative painting techniques into portraiture. The non-academic style that evolved was also influenced by the overriding preference of American patrons for 'correct likenesses' and so it might well be called pragmatic or decorative portraiture.

This catalog accompanies an exhibition of the same name and it is organized to parallel the exhibition. In the installation, the portraits have been grouped in three sections, *A Time of Portraits, Taking a Likeness*, and *A Portrait of Rural Society*, offering a fresh view of New England portraiture and a complement to the Museum's interpretation of a re-created village.

As noted, the National Endowment for the Humanities played a key role in supporting the planning and implementation of this exhibition. We would especially thank Dr. Timothy Meagher, Program Officer, Division of General Programs. Among the individuals and institutions who have provided invaluable assistance are Georgia Barnhill and Thomas Knoles (American Antiquarian Society); Rutheva Brockett; Gail Colglazier (Connecticut Valley Historical Museum); Yoram Szekely, Nancy Harm, and Nancy Jarzombek (Cornell University); Robert Kaufman (Deerfield Academy); David Proper and Suzanne Flynt (Pocumtuck Valley Memorial Association); Elfreda Altobelli, (Forbush Memorial Library); William Hamill, Susan Hamill; Brian Cullity (Heritage Plantation of Sandwich); Stuart P. Feld, (Hirschl and Adler Gallery); Maureen Harper (Museum of our

National Heritage); Bruce MacLeish and Kathleen Stocking (New York State Historical Association); Eloise Beal and Pauline Mitchell (Shelburne Museum); Darrell McGuigan and the Short family; Linda Muehlig, Louise Laplante (Smith College Museum of Art); Martha Hoppin and Karen Papineau (Springfield Museum of Fine Arts); Ruth Hopfman (Sterling Historical Society); William Wallace and Wallis Darnley (Worcester Historical Museum); and William Warren. We acknowledge our gratitude to each of these and the other private lenders, archivists, librarians, and curators, who have cheerfully and promptly assisted us.

Insights and enthusiasm were provided by project consultants, Vincent Ciulla, David Jaffee, Elizabeth Kornhauser, Frank Miele, and Steven Nissenbaum. They worked with our staff planning committee, Sarah Carnahan, John Curtis, Jack Larkin, Margaret Piatt, Bill Reid, Mark Sammons, and Eric White. Interns Allison Kinney, sponsored by Yankee Magazine and the National Trust, and Beverly Johnson gave invaluable research support in the early stages. The production of this catalog was assisted by the patient and supportive staff of the Old Sturbridge Village Research Library, Museum photographers Tom Neill and Henry Peach, copy editor, Roger Parks and Elizabeth Pols of North Pols Design. When it came down to all the details which make an exhibition possible, Donna Baron, Registrar and Curator of Collections, and David Colglazier, Conservator, must be recognized for their efficiency and energy.

Jessica Nicoll and Caroline Sloat

THE FACES OF CHANGE

Images of Self & Society in New England 1790-1850

Jack Larkin

CHARLES BIRD KING'S "THE ITINERANT ARTIST" (fig. 1) shows a travelling painter hard at work on the likeness of a country matron. Recalling his own early years as a portraitist, King has created a densely populated rendering of a rural household. The father and husband is heading out the door, leaving eleven others to watch or participate in the artist's performance. There are eight children, ranging from a grown-up young woman to an infant in the cradle, and a young African-American girl, probably a domestic. An older woman, most likely a widowed grandmother, leans over the canvas to offer constructive criticism.

There was an explosion in the painting of such portraits throughout New England between 1800 and 1850. Thousands of rural and urban families became, like the one King depicts, eager consumers of these likenesses. King presents only one of many versions of sitter and situation; husbands posed as well as wives, children as well as adults, the young and elderly as well as the middle-aged.[1]

Produced by artisan painters,

Fig. 1. Detail of Plate 11, Charles Bird King, The Itinerant Artist.

these portraits were a far-off outwash of the great stream of western European art. Most of the men and women who posed for and purchased these pictures seem to have regarded them as products of artisanry rather than art; this created enormous frustrations for the region's most talented and ambitious artists, opened up opportunities for the less skillful, and has led to a protracted 20th-century debate about the aesthetic merit and cultural meaning of these works.[2]

The faces that look out at us from the paintings of artists such as Joseph Whiting Stock or William Matthew Prior are those of comparatively anonymous men and women. These New Englanders were the first large group of ordinary Americans to have left visual representations behind. Who were they, and what do their likenesses tell us about the world in which they lived? *Meet Your Neighbors: New England Portraits, Painters and Society, 1790-1850*, suggests several different answers to these questions. This essay considers the iconography and social imagery of these paintings—the meaning of their objects and emblems and the ages, status and family linkages of their subjects.

With the passage of the years, these portraits—which ultimately numbered in at least the several thousands—met a variety of fates. Some served for a time as important links between generations before they faded into dimly remembered ancestral images. Others became anonymous, completely dissociated from their original social meanings. Many, perhaps most, have not even survived. But not one of these paintings was a disembodied image at the time of its making. Each represented a definable individual within his or her social milieu, as a memorial, a token of celebration, or a symbol of achievement.

If portraits were our only evidence about New Englanders' lives we would not know much. We would try to decode them like ancient inscriptions, emerging with many hypotheses and little information. But the lives of ordinary people in New England are well documented in comparison with those in most places and times. The portraits, and the evidence about their subjects, makers, and contexts, can illuminate each other. However, much of this is uncharted territory. The multitude of existing likenesses of New England's people has been only partially described and even less well researched.[3]

Earlier, in the 17th and 18th centuries, portraits had been a clear badge of high status in New England, distinguishing magistrates, powerful clergymen, great merchants, country squires, and other members of the elite from ordinary people. However, in the years after 1800, itinerant artists and their customers were beginning to alter the terms of this social equation. Comparatively inexpensive and simple portraits were becoming much more widely available. Probate inventories, the best evidence about the material life of early American families, strongly suggest that in colonial New England there had been few pictures of any kind and no portraits in the great majority of households. In the early 19th century, by contrast, there was a massive increase in the number of known painters and surviving paintings. Inventory studies for a number of central Massachusetts communities from 1800 to 1840 show that the proportion of households with "pictures" of any kind doubled, from less than one in ten to one in five. It seems likely that the ownership of portraits increased several-fold during this time.[4]

Even a casual scanning of a selection of early-19th-century portraits and their subjects discloses that portraiture's view of society was broadening well beyond a small elite. Rural merchants, country doctors, successful house carpenters, and their families were now among those who could claim title to enduring self-images, likenesses that would fix their features on canvas through their own lives and for posterity. This was a very real democratization of the constituency for portraiture, but nonetheless a partial one. Charles

Bird King's painting emphasizes the rusticity of his portrait-sitting family; but, even as a young itinerant, virtually all of his subjects would have been from comfortably prosperous households.[5]

A careful analysis of the biographies of documented portrait sitters indicates that they were for the most part the prosperous, upper-middling beneficiaries of New England's economic transformation in the early 19th century. The patrons or customers of the non-academic painters were not the "folk" living in traditional houses deep in the countryside, but merchants, physicians, lawyers, clergymen, ship captains, manufacturers, the most successful farmers and artisan-proprietors, and their wives and children. In country villages and cities alike, these prosperous but not quite wealthy New Englanders shared tastes, incomes and material standards. Given their actual numbers in the social structure, farmers, craftsmen, and their families were greatly under-represented.

The portraits in oils produced by such artists as Stock, Prior, and Fuller were far less expensive than the academic exemplars that wealthy and aesthetically demanding people continued to commission. Charles Bird King's paintings of Delia Ellsworth Taintor and Henry Taintor (cats. 75, 76), which he produced in his successful artistic maturity, cost $100—five to ten times the price of non-academic portraits, and equivalent to half of a farm laborer's yearly earnings. Even ordinary paintings, however, were not inexpensive when measured against early 19th-century wages and prices. A $10 portrait was worth a week's salary for a country clergyman in the 1830's, and a set of family members' portraits—four or five paintings—could run to $40 or more, enough to purchase a good horse or even rent a house for a year.[6]

If portraits still served to demarcate social boundaries, though, the lines were now less precise and reached farther "down" into the social order. The new portraiture depicted aspiration and respectability rather than authority and power. Frederick Kilner (cat. 50; pl. 23) of Barre, Massachusetts, for example, is painted in flawlessly cut coat, immaculate shirt, and elegant cravat. His identity, hinted at by these stylish clothes, is firmly established by his prominently displayed trade journal: Kilner was not a gentleman of means but a merchant tailor. In the 18th century such a tradesman might have dressed a wealthy man for a portrait sitting, but would never have imagined commissioning one himself. Nancy and William Lawson (cats. 53, 54; pls. 2, 3) of Boston posed confidently for their portraits around 1840; both appear poised and well-dressed. But they were "black Yankees"; Lawson's business as a retail clothing merchant made them members of Boston's small African-American middle class.

In some important ways, portraits were very much like many of the "consumer goods" that were appearing in increasing quantity in early 19th-century New England households: carpets, matched sets of chairs, parlor stoves, framed mirrors, and sofas. These paintings, although not yet mass-produced, were to some extent standardized in format and price. They were bought and sold, most commonly for cash, but often through the networks of exchange that long remained part of rural economic life. And they ranked high among the items of household furniture that defined a "genteel" pattern of material life.[7]

Portraits though, unlike other household furnishings, were images of the self, far more fixed, permanent, and public than those provided by the looking glasses that hung in virtually every New England parlor. Their very existence is testimony to social and economic change, and they are images rich with significance as representations of age, gender, and family relationship, of occupation and class, of social authority and marginality.

ICONOGRAPHY:
REPRESENTATIONS OF RESPECTABILITY

ALONG WITH THE EXPANDED social range of the new portraiture went a democratized and simplified iconography. Most portrait sitters and purchasers expected representations that caught the likeness of their features—a judgment, they were confident, that untrained observers could make. In addition, they usually expected to be depicted with objects that were familiar parts of their everyday lives. Backgrounds, symbols, and properties in these paintings varied to some extent with the preferences of the artist and the idiosyncrasies of the subject. But in a more important way they functioned as conventions of representation, a system of shared meanings and symbols, usually linked with the characteristics of gender, age, occupation, and family role.[8]

The visual language of these portraits was an array of everyday objects and the details of dress. Objects connoting aristocratic lineage, magisterial power or gentlemanly pursuits were replaced by more prosaic symbols. Thus Lewis Baldwin (cat. 8) of Milford, Connecticut, posed for his portrait in 1841 holding a shoe size measure. This was a humble object, but one symbolizing the new sources of wealth that economic change had brought. In 1840, boot and shoe making ranked second only to the production of textiles among the industries that had already made New England a great manufacturing region. Shoe manufacturers such as Baldwin were the organizing entrepreneurs of mass production.

Destined themselves to be items of household furniture, portraits often mirrored the increasingly comfortable abundance of their subjects' domestic interiors. After 1820, portrait sitters were frequently shown seated on painted chairs. These items, mass-produced in New England shops, not only added visual interest to pictures, but were also available by the dozen in prosperous households. Other subjects sat at mahogany-veneered tables or on scroll-arm sofas, or were pictured against the background of figured Brussels carpets. Inventory studies identify these furnishings as emerging emblems of the prosperous American parlor. Pocket watches, either prominently displayed or more genteelly hinted at by watch fobs, often appeared as more personalized icons of prosperity. All of these objects, like the paintings themselves, had earlier been far more restricted in their social range.[9]

Many portraits reflected both New England's traditional commitment to the printed word and a powerful early-19th-century expansion of book production, reading, and access to information. Books, newspapers, periodicals, and the related tools of literacy—letters, sheets of writing paper, accounts, quill pens, and writing tables—were the most commonly used symbols in the portraits of men and women alike. But men were frequently shown in the act of writing or in the pursuit of information, while women were almost always portrayed in a receptive role: holding a book, or reading a letter rather than writing one. Women's books were usually small volumes, sometimes clearly suggesting a New Testament or a work of devotion. Even as portraits registered the quickening pace of early-19th-century commerce and communications, they portrayed women as recipients. Harriet Skerry (cat. 69) of Oakham, Massachusetts, like other postmasters' wives, is shown with an addressed letter in her hands, while her husband Ebenezer poses among his ledgers. It must be admitted that most of these objects were relatively easy to draw and gave imperfectly trained artists something to do with sitters' hands. But they would never have become so widespread in iconography if they had not been part of the common cultural currency of a society in which an unprecedently large number of people had expanding access to printed materials and the flow of information.[10]

A significant number of men's portraits displayed emblems of the work that shaped masculine identity. The likenesses of many merchants (cats. 48, 52, 70) showed them surrounded by their account books and business papers. This evoked the careful record keeping and the reckoning of profit and loss that were part of the storekeeper's world, as well as the mercantile thrust that drove the creation of an expanding network of trade and production. A successful cotton manufacturer such as Isaac Saunders of Saundersville, Rhode Island, might pose for his portrait at home, but with the mill he built and ran conspicuously visible from the window behind him. Lawyers (cat. 56), physicians (cat. 72), and clergymen (cat. 61) are often portrayed as if in their offices or studies, with law reports and commentaries, medical tomes, or theological treatises prominently displayed. The portrait of Jesse Kittredge Smith, a New Hampshire physician, virtually drowns its onlookers in a sea of professional detail (pl. 20). Dr. Smith sits in his office with an array of drugs and surgical instruments spread out on the table beside him. Through a bit of pictorial license, the office's exterior, and the horse-drawn chaise he used on his rounds, are visible through the window. So sharply are all these items rendered that Smith's likeness is the least interesting part of the picture; his features are overwhelmed by the artifacts of his profession.

Artisans' portraits were considerably rarer than those of men in commerce and the professions. But those that were commissioned frequently showed formally dressed men posing with the tools of their trades (cats. 8, 36, 50). Watchmakers and clockmakers held gears or delicate instruments, carpenters grasped their try squares. Occasionally the occupational clue was subtler. Jesse Hartshorn, a master builder of Portland, Maine, was depicted without tools but with a muscular right hand far too prominently displayed to be accidental. But artisans were virtually never depicted in their workshops.

Farmers' portraits were even less common than craftsmen's. Although still the largest occupational group in New England as late as 1850, they were enormously underrepresented in paintings. This was partly because wealth in New England was accumulating considerably faster in commercial and manufacturing pursuits than in agriculture. But the gap between city or village and the open countryside was also one of accessibility and cultural predisposition. Families living in transportation and communication centers, whether large or small, were far more likely to have acquaintance with a whole range of cultural possibilities, portrait painting among them. Strikingly, farmers' painted images contained virtually no reference to agriculture. Ploughs, scythes, and other tools of cultivation almost never appeared, nor were farm landscapes visible from windows. A prosperous Vermont farmer Mark White Adams (cat. 3), for example, is shown holding a wallet, an emblem not of his agricultural routine but of his commercial dealings as a cattle drover. The artist David Bowdoin, who had grown up on a central Massachusetts farm, portrayed his father James (cat. 18; pl. 25), who had worked in his fields all his life, holding a Bible. Portraiture seems to have shared the conviction of an emerging middle-class culture that there was something irredeemably ungenteel about farming, its tools suggesting only back-breaking labor and boots spattered with manure.[11]

Changes in the iconography of ministers' portraits reflected a great transition in social role. Nathanael Howe (cat. 44) was the pastor of an ordinary country church, but his portrait echoes a long tradition of high-style ministerial portraiture, showing him in linen bands and flowing Geneva gown—symbols of clerical authority that Congregational clergymen had worn since the 17th century. Yet Howe was almost an anachronism, a member of New England's last generation of pastors settled for life with wide authority in their communities. The Reverend John Perrin (cat. 61) of Maine, by contrast, is painted in a simple black cravat and tailcoat that had been adopted by virtually all New England clergymen of every denomination by 1830, and is portrayed writing amid his books. Ministers' lives changed enormously when they and their congregations abandoned the expectation of permanence and power. As they took up careers that consisted of a sequence of short-term pastorates, they came to dress, and to be painted, as essentially indistinguishable from other professional men.

A portrait's iconography sometimes provides a glimpse of a virtually unknown social world. At first glance Augustus Fuller's paintings of Edwards Whipple Denny (cat. 25; pl. 9) and Elizabeth Stone Denny (cat. 24; pl. 8) are conventionally symmetrical renderings of husband and wife. But closer scrutiny reveals that he holds a pencil and she a slate, objects that stood for both their literacy and their deafness and were their primary medium for communication with the "hearing world" around them.

Gender roles within the family were also sometimes emphasized by the portrayal of parallel symbols of male occupation and female domesticity. In one sharply delineated portrait pair, Susan Knight (cat. 51) holds her first child, while her husband Asa (cat. 52) is immersed in his papers and accounts. The Knight portraits are an iconographic statement of the early 19th-century social doctrine of "separate spheres" for the sexes. Susan Knight's highly visible identification with motherhood contrasts sharply with her husband's absorption with business.[12]

Fig. 2. S.A. and R.W. Shute, Elizabeth Piper, 1833, oil on canvas, 29 x 24 1/2 (73.6 x 62.3), Old Sturbridge Village. On the reverse, "No. 15. Painted by S.A. and R.W. Shute, January 11, 1833 for Elizabeth Piper, Peterborough, N.H." Piper's name does not appear in the public records of Peterborough. At some point, probably in the 1840s, the full sleeves and wide white collar of the 1830s were overpainted, narrowing the sleeves and adding a black lace collar.

Painted to hang in the parlor, portraits usually placed their female subjects there as well. If men were often depicted at work, women were almost always shown ready to receive company. Their likenesses were much poorer than men's in the emblems of occupation, but far richer in the depiction of dress and adornment. Women's portraits abounded in the detailed renderings of hairstyles and false curls, pins and earrings, embroidered collars and caps, the textures of fabrics and the shapes of sleeves and bodices. As sitters, women collaborated with painters to portray their sense of fashion, their skill in dressmaking, and the quality of their decorative needlework—as well as the prosperity of their husbands. The portrait of Elizabeth Piper of Peterborough, New Hampshire (figure 2), explicitly links feminine skill and elegant dress. She is depicted with a prominently displayed embroidery frame; the pattern of the delicate needlework on the frame matches that of her decorative collar and sleeves.[13]

As for women's activities, portraits again depicted only a limited range of genteel tasks appropriate to the parlor. Occasionally a mother—like Susan Knight, or Fanny Negus

Fuller (cat. 33)—was shown holding a decorously dressed baby. More often women posed next to a sewing table or held their sewing or embroidery. The portrait of Dr. Jesse Kittredge Smith's wife, Permelia (cat. 71; pl. 20), provides a rich inventory of sewing accoutrements, creating an elaborately detailed domestic material world to match his medical one. Considerably more common were simpler depictions of work in hand, as in the portraits of Philena Allbee Adams (cat. 2; pl. 14), shown holding her knitting, or Hannah Chandler Perry (cat. 62), depicted with her thimble. But less seemly processes of housework and child rearing, like the grubby realities of the farm and shop, went unpictured.

Children's portraits turned the focus away from their subjects' unformed faces to full-length renderings of childish body proportions and clothing which used a distinctive iconography. Children, as well as adults, were often portrayed with books, but in other ways were rendered with a clearly different pictorial vocabulary that was closely connected to traditional high-style portraiture. Pets and toys marked off gender-specific realms of play (cats. 5, 37, 57). Boys were usually painted with dogs, connoting outdoor play, sport and hunting; girls were customarily depicted with cats, or small lap-dogs, linked to indoor pursuits and domesticity. Boys were often depicted holding whips, knives, and hammers—the first a fossilized symbol of mastery, the others tools for the application of physical force. Girls were portrayed wearing coral beads, clutching flowers or holding dolls—objects that presaged later ornamental and nurturing roles.[14]

Full-length and thus providing more pictorial space, children's portraits often provided more complete renderings of their families' domestic world than did "head and shoulders" depictions of adults. Children were shown standing on figured parlor carpets, leaning against upholstered furniture, or, in the case of Mary Perry (cat. 65), the daughter of a highly successful tin manufacturer, holding the commercially produced toys which more than anything else signified childhood among the affluent.

The four portraits of members of the Goddard family of Nashua, New Hampshire (cats. 35-38), demonstrate an iconographic scheme that defines family roles and links its members. Nathan W. Goddard is depicted with his watchmaker's tools. His wife Mary is shown facing him and holding a book, the icon of literacy as well as a traditional token of piety and moral seriousness. Sons John and Franklin are also painted facing each other. John, at age six, grasps a book which links him to his mother and also identifies him as a schoolboy. Franklin, age four, clutches a hammer. As a tool, an emblem of manual skill and masculine strength, it connects him to his father, but in his small hands it is clearly a toy, standing for play rather than serious work.

SOCIAL IMAGERY:
PORTRAITS AND THE PATTERNS OF LIFE

REFLECTING ON THE transition from painting to daguerreotypy in 1846, an American writer thought that the primary social impulse of portrait painting had been to bind the generations (fig.3). "At the earnest solicitation of all the junior members of his household," a patriarch might have himself "done upon canvass"; "elderly gentlemen" and "ladies of certain ages" were the primary subjects, he said, whose portraits were taken so that their children would be able to gaze reverentially at "the lineaments of lost parents."[15] But tabulations of portrait subjects' age, sex and family connections, based on currently available documentation, suggest that the social roles embodied in portraiture were much more complex.

The non-academic portraiture of the early 19th century did not aim primarily at providing images of a soon-to-depart elder generation. For adults, the distribution of portrait subjects by age roughly mirrored the age structure of New England society as a whole. Men and women in their 50s, 60s, and 70s were depicted in documented paintings in approximately the same small proportions as their numbers in the total adult population. There were more likenesses of people in their 20s than in their 30s, more of either than those in their 40's, and so on; this paralleled the "age pyramid" of New England's population, whose still high birth rates and significant mortality for young and middle-aged adults made it much younger than our own.[16]

Fig. 3. Frederick R. Spencer, Family Group, 1840, oil on canvas, 29 3/16 x 36 (74 x 91.5) The Brooklyn Museum: Dick S. Ramsay Fund.

Nor was New England portraiture a celebration of youth, although the eyes of contemporary viewers may well have been drawn, as the interests of 20th-century collectors frequently are, to past likenesses of children. Adults seem clearly to have predominated as subjects. Compared to their large numbers in New England families and communities, children were substantially under-represented. Those under 18 constituted about 45% of New England's population in 1830, but made up no more than 20% of the documented subjects of portraits.

The mothers of very young children only rarely had their babies or toddlers included in their portraits. About one married woman in twenty was so portrayed, a much lower proportion than the facts of the birth rate and family structure would suggest. In the communities of mid-19th-century Massachusetts, about one married woman in five had a child two years old or under.

Within the universe of portrayed childhood there seem to have been sharp distinctions of age. Younger children were substantially more likely to be painted than older ones. From 1834 to 1845 Joseph Whiting Stock (figs.4,5) clearly noted the occasions on which he painted children, and recorded the ages of the great majority of them. Most of Stock's child subjects were very young: almost half under five years of age, and most of the rest under ten. Young people between the ages of 11 and 16 were greatly underrepresented; Stock's records suggest that these older children were the least likely of all New Englanders to be painted.

Such a preference for the very young may have been rooted in demographic reality. In terms of exposure to illness and the risks of death, these were the most vulnerable years, as parents unavoidably knew. The images of babyhood and early childhood were precious because they were precarious. Parents could be more confident, although far from certain, of seeing an older child through to adulthood.[17]

This interpretation is strengthened by the finding that a significant number of children's images were overtly commissioned as memorial pictures — that is, artifacts of mourning.

Far more often than when an adult died, early-19th-century families that had lost a child would summon a portrait artist, if one were nearby, to the bereaved household in order to take a likeness "from the corpse." Nearly one-fifth of Stock's paintings of children, for example, were posthumous—a figure that roughly coincides with the total proportion of young New Englanders dying between birth and adulthood; fewer than one in a hundred of his portraits of adults were memorial pictures.

The relative scarcity of late childhood portraits contrasts strikingly with the abundance of those of young adults. New Englanders were far more likely to become portrait subjects as they crossed the threshold of young womanhood in their late teens or young manhood in their early 20s. A number of these portraits of young adults were commissioned by their families, although some found their way into a son's or daughter's household after marriage. Others were painted during courtship. Stock's accounts for his stay in New Bedford, Massachusetts, for example, reveal this pattern when they are linked to the community's marriage records. In April of 1843, Joseph Ward, a young clothing merchant and tailor, commissioned portraits of himself and his mother, the artist "to take pay from his shop." Two weeks later Stock began a portrait of Caroline Fessenden, and was again "to receive pay of Mr. Ward." In June, Stock undertook likenesses of stable owner James Paul and dressmaker Maria Wilcox. A few months later, Joseph and Caroline were married to each other, as were James and Maria. Each of these portrait pairs marked a successful courtship and surely became prominent objects in the newlyweds' homes. [18]

Fig. 4. Joseph Whiting Stock, Self portrait, c.1843, oil on artist's board, 10 x 8 (25.4 x 20.3), Connecticut Valley Historical Museum. Unable to walk after a childhood accident, Joseph Whiting Stock became a successful portraitist in the 1830s and 1840s. His journal, kept between 1834 and 1846, provides the fullest account yet discovered of an early-19th-century New England portrait painter's subjects, output, and prices; its autobiographical preface describes how he learned his craft and became self-supporting.

Portraits most often took their social meaning from the constellation of family relationships. The majority were the likenesses of husbands, wives, daughters and sons, destined for display in the family's parlor or sitting room and commissioned and paid for by the head of the household.

Portrait pairs—the complementary images of a married couple—accounted for one-third to fully one-half of all the paintings. Husbands and wives were not often depicted on the same canvas, but their connection was virtually always indicated by identical backgrounds, mirrored poses, and symmetrically arranged furnishings. These paintings—of couples ranging in age from their early 20s through their 70's—confirmed, even celebrated, the conjugal bond as the foundation of society. Some families, of course, chose to commission a single portrait—father's, mother's, child's—for economic or idiosyncratically personal reasons that may well forever elude discovery.

Portraits of larger family groups were as unusual as the joint images of married couples. But family sequences of individual paintings were very common. Nearly a quarter of Joseph Whiting Stock's output of portraits, for example, was commissioned in groupings of three or more: these usually were likenesses of father, mother and at least one child, but sometimes included a sibling or parent of husband or wife. The predominance of single portraits over group images should not be taken as reflecting the triumph of individualism over family cohesion. A series of individual portraits was less likely to be taxing to the artisan painter's compositional skills than a larger-scale canvas, and smaller paintings may well have fit more comfortably into the furnishing schemes of parlors and sitting rooms.

Fig. 5. O.H. Cooley, Joseph Whiting Stock, daguerreotype, 1843-6, Connecticut Valley Historical Museum. Stock is shown with his sister Lucy S. Gould, who had accompanied him on some of his painting trips before her marriage. Although Stock formed business associations with daguerreotypists, he did not take up the new technology himself and continued to paint portraits in substantial numbers up to his death in 1855.

The evidence also suggests that there was some change over time in the social dimensions of portraiture. Paintings commissioned outside the family by single men and women may have become increasingly significant in the 1830s and 40s, reflecting an array of changes in occupations, cultural opportunities, and living arrangements.[19]

For some young men and women—perhaps especially those who attended widely available lyceum lectures on the moral significance of art—commissioning and sitting for a portrait could be an act of self-assertion and cultural aspiration. There was a diverse and expanding multitude of private "secondary" schools in early 19th-century New England, and teaching in them became a significant occupation, particularly for men and women in transition, whose lives had not yet settled down. The young teachers of the new Wesleyan Academy in Wilbraham, Massachusetts, twice invited Joseph Whiting Stock to stay at the school, in 1836 and 1837. During his visits seven teachers (four men and three women) sat for portraits, and he also painted several portrait pairs and sequences of children for families in the community. The images of teachers went to hang, at least at first, not in family parlors but in the austere quarters of a country school's dormitory. [20]

New England's factory operatives were also clearly beginning to sit for portraits as well. In the years after 1825, textile manufacturing communities were becoming increasingly full of young single women with their own money to spend. When the painter Augustus Fuller passed through Lowell in 1843, he noted that there were opportunities for "painting beautiful girls in mills and factories"; some of them were "very remarkable beautiful and smart with money plenty." On his visits to Cabotville, a fast-growing "factory village" on the outskirts of Springfield, Stock painted numerous portraits of young women whom he referred to in his journal as "Miss"; the great majority of Cabotville's large female population had come there to work in the cotton mills. Many of New England's mill workers strove to dress fashionably and to live as "genteelly" as possible given their exhausting hours; clearly, there were portraits decorating boarding house bedchambers or their tiny collective parlors—or sent back to the family home as a gift. The portrait of Sarah Shedd (cat. 68; pl.13) of New Hampshire is one of the few surviving documented likenesses of these young women who left their farm homes to work in the textile factories, but there were certainly many more; most such portraits were probably incorporated into their sitters' families of marriage, and their "mill girl" identities were lost.[21]

Even adjusted for their proportion of the population—about 6% of men and 10% of women over 40 were unmarried in representative Massachusetts communities in 1850—portraits of lifelong bachelors or single women are rare indeed among documented paintings. Those without conjugal ties may well have had fewer reasons to be painted in the first place. And even for those who did commission paintings preservation was apt to be poorer, since they lacked direct descendants to inherit and value their portraits. Such underrepresentation probably also reflects the marginal economic and social status of unmarried people in 19th-century America. The joint portrait of the Adams sisters (cat. 1), of Manchester, New Hampshire, along with the portrait of Sarah Shedd, stand out as the rare images of those who lived out their lives outside the dominant family pattern.

THE ICONOGRAPHY AND SOCIAL IMAGERY of New England's non-academic portraiture require more comprehensive study. A great deal of work is still needed in analyzing artists' records, identifying and documenting paintings, and decoding their cultural meanings. But even this brief exploration suggests that portraits can tell us much about how New England's people sought to portray themselves, their families, their material lives, and their aspirations. Artifacts of a society in rapid transition, these likenesses were truly faces of change.

---

[1] See David Jaffee, "The Age of Democratic Portraiture," and Elizabeth Mankin Kornhauser, "Staring Likenesses," in this volume. Also see Jaffee, "One of the Primitive Sort: Portrait Makers of the Rural North, 1760-1860," in Steven Hahn and Jonathan Prude, eds., *The Countryside in the Age of Capitalist Transformation* (Chapel Hill: The University of North Carolina Press, 1985), 103-138.

[2] This essay assumes that portraits can and should be studied—although not exclusively—as commercially produced objects and as powerful social images. See Marcia Pointon, "Portrait Painting as a Business Enterprise in London in the 1780s," *Art History*, 7 (June, 1984): 187-205, and Laurel Fecych Sprague, ed., *Agreeable Situations: Society, Commerce and Art in Southern Maine, 1780-1830* (Kennebunk, Maine, 1987). Not everyone agrees. Frank J. Miele et. al., "Folk, or Art?: A Symposium," *Antiques*, 135 (1989): 272-287, displays the widely divergent views of connoisseurs and contextually oriented scholars. The social and cultural meanings of ordinary paintings are discussed in John Michael Vlach, *Plain Painters: Making Sense of American Folk Art* (Washington: Smithsonian Institution Press, 1988); *Folk Art and Art Worlds: Essays Drawn from the Washington Meeting on Folk Art*, Vlach and Simon Bronner, eds. (Ann Arbor: University of Michigan Research Press,

1986); Kenneth L. Ames, *Beyond Necessity: Art in the Folk Tradition* (Winterthur, Del.: Henry Francis du Pont Winterthur Museum, 1977), and "Folk Art: The Challenge and the Promise," in *Perspectives on American Folk Art*, Ian M. G. Quimby and Scott T. Swank, eds., (New York: W. W. Norton & Co., 1979), 293-324.

[3] See Lillian B. Miller, "The Puritan Portrait: Its Function in Old and New England," in *Seventeenth-Century New England*, David D. Hall and David Grayson Allen, eds., (Boston: The Colonial Society of Massachusetts, 1984), 153-84; Elizabeth Mankin Kornhauser, "Painting and Other Pictorial Arts," in *The Great River: Art and Society in the Connecticut River Valley, 1635-1820* (Hartford, Conn.: The Wadsworth Atheneum, 1985), 135-141.

[4] This discussion is based primarily on research undertaken at Old Sturbridge Village [hereafter O.S.V.] in the following collections of records: Probate Inventories for the towns of Brimfield, Palmer, Chester, Sturbridge, Shrewsbury and Barre, Massachusetts, 1790-1850; Probate Inventory Sample of Worcester County Farmers, Mechanics and Merchants, 1790-1850. Originals, Worcester and Hampden County Courthouses, Worcester and Springfield, Massachusetts; transcripts and analyses, Research Department, O.S.V.. See also Abbott Lowell Cummings, *Rural Household Inventories*

1675-1775 (Boston: Society for the Preservation of New England Antiquities, 1964), and Kornhauser, "Painting and Other Pictorial Arts."

Discussions of the number and range of pictorial objects in New England households are subject to considerable uncertainty. Probate inventories are the only systematic evidence available for the study of the domestic environment, but what they contain, and what they leave out, is not always clear. In the probate practices of some communities, paintings may have been skipped altogether, perhaps because they were conventionally considered non-economic goods or were too difficult for the assessors to value. It may also have been relatively common for family members to have taken paintings before the estate inventory was taken. However, 18th- and 19th-century New England inventories do record significant numbers of "pictures" in a minority of households; virtually all mentioned pictures were recorded in estates in the upper 10-20% of wealth-holding. The recorded value of images varied greatly; in those relatively rare instances when "portraits" were specifically mentioned, they were given greater value than other pictures, many of which may have been engravings.

The inventory evidence probably undercounts the number of "pictures", but it is not clear by how much. In 1850 there were at least 500,000 households in New England; if there were portraits in 1 house in 10, there would then have been at least 50,000 portrait paintings in existence in the region—and perhaps more, given the prevalence of pairs and family sequences. Although there are no estimates of the total output of pre-1850 New England portraiture, it seems unlikely to be larger than this figure.

If most New England households were not displaying paintings and engravings, it is certain that other images— silhouettes, family records, pieces of "schoolgirl" art produced by family members—were considerably more common. Particularly if they were unframed, such items were unlikely to have been inventoried because they had never been purchased or had minimal market value.

[5] This essay's statements on iconography and social imagery are based on the following sources: documented portraits in the O.S.V. permanent collection; documented portraits assembled for the "Meet Your Neighbors" exhibit; published documented portraits in the following studies: Mary Black, Barbara C. and Lawrence B. Holdridge, *Ammi Phillips: Portrait Painter 1788-1865* (New York: Clarkson N. Potter, 1969); Jacquelyn Oak et. al., *Face to Face: M.W. Hopkins and Noah North* (Lexington, Mass.: Museum of Our National Heritage, 1988); Mary Black, *Erastus Salisbury Field 1805-1900* (Springfield, Mass.: Springfield Museum of Fine Arts, 1984); and *The Paintings and the Journal of Joseph Whiting Stock*, Juliette Tomlinson, ed. (Middletown, Conn.: Wesleyan University Press, 1976), which includes Stock's detailed record of portrait subjects, locations, sizes and prices between 1834 and 1846. Data on gender, age, occupation, family relationship, iconography, and portrait grouping and cost was tabulated from these sources and analyzed. Detailed tables are available in Jack Larkin, "Ordinary New England Portraiture: A Preliminary Statistical Inquiry," unpublished paper, 1991, O.S.V. Research Department.

All paintings discussed in this essay are reproduced in this volume; they are referred to in the text by catalog entry or figure number.

[6] For most of his individual portraits in the years 1834-46,

Joseph Whiting Stock charged between $8 and $10. Smaller paintings were sometimes priced as low as $4; rarer large canvases, often with two subjects, generally cost $15 to $20 with a few as high as $30. For wages and prices in early-19th-century America, see Stanley Lebergott, *Manpower in American Economic Growth: The American Record since 1800* (New York: McGraw-Hill, 1964), 257-304 and appendix; Dorothy Brady, "Consumption and the Style of Life," in Lance E. Davis, et al., *American Economic Growth: An Economist's History of the United States* (New York: Harper and Row, 1972), 61-85; O.S.V. Research Department files on wages, salaries, prices and taxable values in rural New England, 1790-1860.

[7] Jaffee, "One of the Primitive Sort," and "The Age of Democratic Portraiture"; Jack Larkin, *The Reshaping of Everyday Life* (New York: Harper & Row, 1988), 116-148.

[8] Karin Calvert, "Children in American Family Portraiture, 1670 to 1810," *William and Mary Quarterly*, 3d ser. 39 (January 1983): 57-113, and Margaretta Lovell, "Reading Eighteenth-Century American Family Portraits: Social Images and Self-Images," *Winterthur Portfolio: A Journal of American Material Culture*, 22 (Winter 1987): 243-264.

[9] Larkin, *Reshaping*, 121-48; Jaffee, "The Age of Democratic Portraiture," this volume; Edgar DeN. Mayhew and Minor Meyers, Jr., *A Documentary History of American Furnishings to 1815* (New York: Scribner's, 1980), 44-123.

[10] For portraits in the *Meet Your Neighbors* exhibit whose iconography includes books or other artifacts of literacy, see: for women, cats. 13, 15, 22, 25, 36, 43, 50, 54, 70, 72; for men, cats. 17, 24, 26, 46, 49, 51, 56, 61, 69; for children, cats. 5, 6, 37. On the early-19th-century revolution in communications and reading, see Richard D. Brown, *Knowledge is Power: The Diffusion of Information in Early America, 1700-1865* (New York: Oxford University Press, 1989), 3-15, 132-296; and William J. Gilmore, *Reading Becomes a Necessity of Life: Material and Cultural Life in Rural New England, 1780-1835* (Knoxville: University of Tennessee Press, 1989).

[11] See Richard L. Bushman, "Opening the American Countryside," in James A. Henretta, Michael Kammen, and Stanley N. Katz, eds., *The Transformation of Early American History: Society, Authority and Ideology* (New York: Alfred G. Knopf, 1991), 239-256, and Jack Larkin, "From 'Country Mediocrity' to 'Rural Improvement': Transforming the Slovenly Countryside in Central Massachusetts, 1775-1840," *Everyday Life in the Early Republic: Winterthur Conference Report Number 29*, Katherine M. Hutchins, ed. (Charlottesville: University of Virginia Press for the Winterthur Museum, forthcoming, 1992).

[12] For early-19th-century New England views on "separate spheres," see Nancy F. Cott, *The Bonds of Womanhood: "Woman's Sphere" in New England 1780-1835* (New Haven: Yale University Press, 1976).

[13] New England room-by-room inventories show the great majority of portraits—and other pictures—to have been in rooms either designated as "parlors" or clearly, from the evidence of other furnishings, performing the functions of the most formal and ceremonial space in the home. See sources in fn. 5.

[14] Calvert, "Children in American Family Portraiture."

[15] Augustine J.H. Duganne, *The Daguerreotype Miniature; or Life in the Empire City* (Philadelphia: G.B. Zieber & Co., 1846), 30.

[16] See Larkin, *Reshaping*, 9-15, 62-104; Maris Vinovskis,

Fertility in Massachusetts from the Revolution to the Civil War (New York: Academic Press, 1981), 11-23; age structure data for New England states and communities, 1830-1850 and for documented portrait sitters are available in Larkin, "Ordinary Rural Portraiture."

[17] Nancy Schrom Dye and Daniel Blake Smith, "Mother Love and Infant Death, 1750-1920," *Journal of American History*, 73 (September 1986): 329-353; Maris Vinovskis, "Mortality in Massachusetts to 1860," *Journal of Economic History*, 32 (March 1972): 184-213; and "Angels Heads and Weeping Willows: Death in Early America," *Proceedings of the American Antiquarian Society*, 86 part 2 (October 1976): 275-302.

[18] *Journal of Joseph Whiting Stock*, 34-39; *Vital Records of New Bedford, Massachusetts to the Year 1850* (Boston: New England Historic Genealogical Society, 1932).

[19] Ammi Phillips's documented paintings for 1811-1835 show very few images of either men or women other than those painted in family groups. Stock's journal indicates that he painted a significant number of young unmarried women living outside their parental households in Wilbraham and Cabotville in the 1830's and 1840's. The data on Phillips's portrait subjects, because it is based on surviving documented portraits, may be biased by the processes of preservation. So little is currently known about the business practices and clientage patterns of New England portraitists that these can only be tentative suggestions.

[20] *Journal of Joseph Whiting Stock*, 12-15, 18-21; David Sherman, *History of the Wesleyan Academy in Wilbraham, Massachusetts 1817-1893* (Boston: McDonald and Gill, 1893), 1-35; Jay Mack Holbrook, comp., *Wilbraham Vital Records 1752-1851* (Oxford, Mass.: Holbrook Research Institute, 1983, microfiche).

[21] Augustus Fuller to George Fuller, January 24, 1843, Fuller-Negus Papers, see cat. 6, fn. 2; *Journal of Joseph Whiting Stock*, 13-14, 18-21, 23; Vera Shlakman, *Economic History of a Factory Town: A Study of Chicopee, Massachusetts*, Smith College Studies in History 20, (1934-35; reprint New York: Octagon Press, 1969), 24-97; George S. White, *Memoir of Samuel Slater* (Philadelphia, 1836), 267; Thomas Dublin, *Women at Work: the Transformation of Work and Community in Lowell, Massachusetts, 1826-1860* (New York: Columbia University Press, 1979).

"STARING LIKENESSES"
Portraiture in Rural New England, 1790-1850

Elizabeth Mankin Kornhauser

THE TASTE FOR PORTRAITURE IN RURAL NEW ENGLAND emerged from a long-established tradition dating back to the 17th century. As early as the 1670s, and continuing for a century and more, portraits, with few exceptions, were the only form of painting sought by Americans. This essay will explore the tradition of portraiture, looking at the artists who helped establish this taste and their influence on 19th-century painting styles.

In the 17th-century a handful of portrait painters in the Boston area were actively producing formal portraits of wealthy merchants, ministers, and members of their families.[1] Boston continued to be the leading center of artistic activity in the 18th century, where the Anglo-American legacy of portraiture was furthered by the arrival of such European-trained painters as John Smibert (1688-1751) and Joseph Blackburn (active in North America, 1753-1763). Boston produced the first great American artist, John Singleton Copley (1738-1815), whose genius would dominate American portraiture throughout the century. And as Boston grew, it became a center for artists and their patrons, for teachers, students, and purveyors of art supplies.

The disruption of society during the American Revolution resulted in an artistic hiatus, which ended with the return of Ralph Earl (1751-1801) to his native country from an eight-

Fig. 6. Ralph Earl, Oliver Ellsworth and Abigail Wolcott Ellsworth, 1792, oil on canvas, 75 15/16 x 86 3/4 (192.9 x 220.3). Gift of the Ellsworth Heirs, Wadsworth Atheneum, Hartford.

year absence in England. One of the first American artists with formal training to resume his activity in New England after the war, Earl was a painter of considerable ability. Travelling as an itinerant artist in rural areas of Connecticut, western Massachusetts, and Vermont in the 1790s, he transformed his British portrait style to suit the simpler tastes of his rural patrons, who desired appropriate images of themselves as citizens of a new republic. In the middle class, Earl found a new clientele for portraiture. *Oliver Ellsworth and Abigail Wolcott Ellsworth* (fig.6), painted in Windsor, Connecticut, in 1792, inspired a burst of pictorial production in Connecticut and western Massachusetts. It influenced Earl's subsequent commissions and inspired numerous imitators.[2]

Fig. 7. Gilbert Stuart, George Washington, 1796, oil on canvas, 96 1/4 x 60 1/4 (244.5 x 153). Pennsylvania Academy of the Fine Arts, Philadelphia. Bequest of William Bingham. The first of several versions painted for Bingham, this is known as the "Lansdowne Washington," as it was sent as a gift to the marquis of Lansdowne. It is currently on loan to the National Portrait Gallery in Washington, D.C.

During the first half of the 19th century, members of rural New England society demonstrated an unprecedented demand for portraiture. By and large, these first-time patrons' understanding of art was limited to their desire for a portrait likeness, painted quickly and cheaply. They viewed art as functional, and portraiture served a variety of useful functions. This preference held throughout much of the century, despite the concerted efforts of many academically trained painters, who had been exposed to the great classics of art in Europe, hoped to elevate the tastes of their fellow countrymen, and waited for an example to establish a national art in the form of history painting and civic portraits of American heroes. John Trumbull (1756-1843) painted his series of Revolutionary War scenes, for example, and Gilbert Stuart (1755-1828) created images for the new nation in the form of civic portraits of George Washington (fig. 7). These works became icons for the era.

The emergence of artists capable of fulfilling the demand for portraits and their methods of producing the desired likenesses are explored in this exhibition. An extraordinary number of early-19th-century portraits have survived. This essay will examine the portraits, the methods and materials used to produce them, and their functions and forms.

During their working lives, artists such as Earl and Stuart influenced the look of portraiture, providing accessible models for their less-trained and less-traveled contemporaries. Stuart established himself initially in New York when he returned from England in 1793. There, the artist William Dunlap observed that "all who admired the art or wished to avail themselves of the artist's talents, daily resorted" to Stuart's Stone Street atelier. It seemed to Dunlap that he had never seen portraits before, "so decidedly was form and mind conveyed to the canvas."[3] Stuart moved to Boston in 1805 and remained there until his death, becoming the leading portrait painter in America, and transforming fashionable portraiture in the nation's urban centers. He favored a bust-length format, and his sophisticated "painterly" style was characterized by rapid, facile brushwork and the subtle blending of color to create a soft atmospheric effect (figs. 8,9).

Many in the next generation of portraitists were significantly affected by Stuart's work. William Matthew Prior (1806-1873) for one, held a lifelong admiration for Stuart. At times, Prior, who named his eldest son after Stuart, aspired to emulate his work. Prior produced copies after Stuart's famous portrait of George Washington that hung in the Boston Atheneum, and in 1831 he allowed his own portrait of Abraham Hammatt [location unknown] to be shown at the annual exhibition of the Boston Atheneum in company with works by Stuart and other leading American artists.[4]

Following Stuart's death, Chester Harding (1792-1866) became New England's lead-

Fig. 8. *Gilbert Stuart, Hannah Sweet Lee Dearborn (Mrs. Henry Alexander Scammell Dearborn), c. 1812, oil on panel, 28 3/8 x 22 7/8 (57.1 x 69.2); Bowdoin College Museum of Art, Brunswick, Me., bequest of Miss Mary J.E. Clapp.*

ing portrait painter, attracting, as had his predecessors, public acclaim and customers. He established his studio in Boston in 1821 and boasted, "my room became a fashionable resort, and I painted the enormous number of eighty heads in six months."[5] Harding later moved to Springfield, Massachusetts.

ARTISTS

THOSE WHO WERE ENCOURAGED BY the growing desire for likenesses to take up the pursuit of portrait painting can be considered in three groups. There were some with formal training, such as Ralph Earl, who chose to spend most of their careers traveling in provincial regions. Others with academic training spent an early stage in their career traveling through small towns gaining reputations that allowed them to establish permanent residence in an urban center. Most of the artists represented in this exhibition belong to a third group, who emerged from an artisan-craft tradition and were essentially self-taught.

This group included a large number of limners who portrayed the rural New England society of the time. They had widely differing levels of skill, training, and ambition. With few exceptions, they pursued itinerant lifestyles, traveling from town to town in search of commissions. They functioned as entrepreneurs, speculating that they would be able to attract customers in the regions to which they journeyed. They often relied on some form of patronage network, family connection, or social entrée. Most offered traditional forms of portraiture that were understood by their patrons, while others succeeded in introducing new forms, altering their styles to suit growing public demand.[6]

Fig. 9. Gilbert Stuart, Major-General Henry Alexander Scammell Dearborn, c. 1812, oil on panel 27 1/4 x 22 1/2 (69.2 x 57.1), Bowdoin College Museum of Art, Brunswick, Me., bequest of Miss Mary J. E. Clapp.

Even with formal training, Ralph Earl spent most of his career traveling in the countryside. Charles Bird King (1785-1862, see cats. 75, 76) also had the benefit of academic training abroad and was a versatile and gifted painter who viewed art in the loftiest terms. When he returned from England in 1812, he faced the difficulty of establishing an artistic career in America and took up the life of an itinerant limner. For seven years, King traveled between his native town of Newport, Rhode Island, and Philadelphia, Richmond, and Washington. By the mid-1820s, he achieved his goal of establishing a permanent residence. He settled in Washington, where he had an impressive house, a "Painting Room," and an "Exhibition room" with a skylight. On a visit to the city in 1824, William Dunlap noted that King was "full of business and a great favorite, assiduously employed in his painting room through the day and in the evening attending the soirees, parties, and balls of ambassadors, secretaries of the cabinet, president or other representatives and servants of the people, and justly esteemed everywhere." He served the American public by painting scenes from history, genre subjects, and still lifes, as well as a variety of portraits. He is, perhaps, most famous for his portraits of native Americans.[7]

Many years later, King recalled the early stage of his career in a genre painting, *The Itinerant Artist*, c.1830 (pl.11). While the rustic room interior demonstrates an obvious debt to 17th-century Dutch art, the painting was in large part autobiographical, providing a revealing testimony of the life and trials of the traveling limner in America. Here King touches on the artist's unorthodox methods of taking a likeness, the chaotic and rustic surroundings of the sitting, and the interchange that took place between the artist and the sitter's extended family. This painting defines the majority of King's artistic contemporaries, who fall within the category of the artisan-painter. Although he had long since abandoned the intinerant life style, King drew on his experience to convey the circumstances faced by most of America's artists.

As an example, Joseph Whiting Stock (1815-1855, figs. 4, 5), of Springfield, Massachusetts, revealed much about himself and his development as a professional itinerant limner in his personal journal, which covers the first fourteen years of his career. Stock was partially paralyzed from a childhood accident, an event which, in his own words, left him "incapable of following pursuits by which most men gain a living [and thus] influenced my course through life." At the suggestion of his family's physician, Stock's "attention was directed to the art of Painting, which [he thought] I might easily attain and support myself by painting portraits."[8] He took a few lessons from a local Springfield painter, Franklin White, who had been a pupil of Chester Harding. During a productive and successful career, which began in 1832, Stock painted over 1000 portraits, together with other genres, including a number of landscapes. Although he received little formal training, what he *was* taught came indirectly from Harding, one of the noted practitioners of the art of portraiture. Ultimately, Stock owned an extensive number of books and manuals, many of them relating to art and artistic instruction. They included Charles Davies, *A Treatise on Shades and Shadows and Linear Perspective* (1832), Chapman's *American Drawing-Book* (1847), and Henry T. Tuckerman's *Artist-Life* (1847).[9]

James Guild's frequently quoted diary documents the transformation of a Vermont farm boy into an artisan painter. In his lively account, Guild describes his involvement from 1818 to 1824 in such varied occupations as a peddler, tinker, wrestler, profile cutter, portrait painter, and penmanship instructor. By his own admission, his earliest effort at taking a portrait (of a young lady) had been preceded by only one day of instruction from a local portrait painter in Canandaigua, New York. By his own admission, too, the result "would not be cal[l]ed painting for it looked more like a strangled cat than it did like her."[10]

As these and other examples noted in the catalog suggest, artists not only demonstrated a broad range of skill and training as a group, but the individual output of each artist over the course of his or her career varied dramatically in quality and style. In 1867 Henry T. Tuckerman observed this discrepancy, claiming that American artists were distinguished from their European counterparts by the uneven quality of their productions. He wrote:

> [I]n America the variations of ability or merit in results of individual art are unparalleled. We can sometimes hardly realize that the same hand is responsible for the various works attributed thereto, so wide is the interval between crudity and finish, expression and indifference....The imperfect training, the pressure of necessity, the hurry and bustle of life, the absence of a just and firm critical influence, and a carelessness which scorns pains-taking as a habit...are among the manifest causes of this remarkable inequality.[11]

Tuckerman's observations would seem an apt description of an artist such as William Matthew Prior (cats. 42,43,53,54,57; pls. 2,3,4), whose works reveal a wide disparity in technical proficiency during his lengthy professional career. In fact, this was an intentional feature of his work, for he was willing to alter his manner of portrait painting and his fee, based on the requirements of his sitter. Thus he successfully attracted a broad clientele in both provincial and urban settings.

Prior began his artistic career in his native state of Maine in the 1820s. Newspaper advertisements appeared in Bath and Portland heralding his skill as an ornamental painter available to do japanning, bronzing, oil gilding, and varnishing, military and sign painting, as well as portraiture.[12]

His self-portrait done in 1825 reveals a confident young man, dressed in the fashions of the day, holding his brush and palette, as if contemplating any necessary finishing touches (pl. 4). The composition of the self-portrait is derived from European tradition. In this painting, Prior conveyed the seriousness of his ambition and the stylistic sophistication of which he was capable. His brushwork is adept and fluid. He uses a subtle palette of muted colors. Ultimately, Prior's understanding of anatomy and his use of light and shade to articulate his facial features combine to produce an impressive early effort.

While Prior suggests to the viewer of this painting his opinion of himself as an accomplished and serious artist, portraiture continued to be only one of the ways in which he worked as a painter, even after he moved to Boston. There he continued to do ornamental painting, such as the decorating of clock faces, and he also undertook periods of itinerancy. The artist established his "Painting Garret" in Boston in 1846, but he had traveled for two years before that and would do so again in the early 1850s. He is known to have worked in such places as Newport, Rhode Island, and Baltimore.

Even when he did paint portraits they were not always as technically proficient as his self-portrait. The price of a Prior portrait depended on the patron's desire and willingness to pay. Those "wishing for a flat picture" could "have a likeness without shade or shadow at one quarter price." By the mid-1840's his price for flat pictures was $2.92 "including Frame, Glass, &c," and they were "done in about an hour's sitting."[13]

A comparison of *Portrait of an Unknown Woman* (cat. 80), which represents Prior's simple flat style, with his *Portrait of Mrs. Hartshorn* (cat. 43), painted in an accomplished academic style, demonstrates the two forms taken by his portraits. The first is a rapid recording of his sitter's facial features. He uses broadly applied primary colors to capture the bare outlines of his subject's face, including an unflattering view of her mouth and teeth. Almost as an afterthought, Prior includes a bust-length view of her upper body, which is proportionally much too small and is squeezed into the lower quarter of the painting. Prior's portrait of Mrs. Hartshorn, on the other hand, is far more sophisticated and painstakingly executed. The sitter is placed in a sensual and animated pose. Prior creates a three-dimensional image of his subject by careful delineation, and the use of light and shade. He also attempts to convey a sense of the sitter's personality in his sensitive likeness of Mrs. Hartshorn.

These two portraits also define the two poles of portraiture described in a manual on oil painting compiled from various European writings on art, which appeared in several editions after 1845. "We aim to help the student become an *artist*, not a dauber," wrote the editor of his attempt to steer aspiring artists away from the manner of flat portraiture represented by *Unknown Woman* and encourage a more accomplished, perceptive, and painstaking method, as evidenced in *Mrs. Hartshorn*.

> There are always certain traits of feature...that are readily seized by a moderately observant eye, and which, when delineated, have the advantage of being universally recognized. These when stiffly set down form what are called *staring likenesses*. The man, or rather, the animal is there, the outward crust, but the immortal part, the interior existence is no where represented."[14]

It would appear, however, as the success of Prior's flat pictures attests, that many rural New Englanders were satisfied with the "staring likeness."

METHODS AND MATERIALS

THE PAINTER'S BACKGROUND, level of training, artistic inclination, and patronage all helped to determine the look of a portrait. His or her methods and materials also played a role in the outcome. Charles Bird King illustrated some of the difficulties encountered by the traveling portraitist in *The Itinerant Artist* (fig. 10). Artists such as the one in this painting often lacked the advantages of a formal studio setting, with appropriate easels, props, and lighting. Instead, as here, they were often at the mercy of their surroundings—in a local tavern, for example, or in a sitter's house. King's artist has placed his subject near a window to catch the available daylight, while he is seated on a stool, holding in his left hand a palette of colors, several paint brushes, and a maul stick (used to steady his hand). He pulls his right hand, holding a brush, back from the canvas to examine his handiwork. A primed canvas has been applied over what may have been either a wooden stretcher (which could be adjusted by keying out) or a strainer (which could not be adjusted). Evidently lacking an easel, he has improvised by propping the canvas on the back of a chair, while his subject is seated precariously on a wooden platform elevated by two logs. A box holding the rest of his pigments, bottles of turpentine, brushes, palette knives and rags, is on the floor.

In many instances the patron paid for the materials used for the portrait and may have been unwilling to purchase the most expensive pigments or fine linen canvas. The painter either had to travel with art materials in hand or rely on the stock of local merchants. Several manuals of the period such as *The Artist and Tradesman's Guide* (1829) were addressed to artists and craftsmen alike,[15] who undoubtedly purchased their supplies from common sources.

Fig. 10. The Itinerant Artist, detail of Pl. 11 showing the tools of the artist's trade: his box of colors, palette, and maul stick.

Artists in rural regions could not obtain the more expensive and up-to-date pigments and must have found these manuals useful allowing them to improvise with fewer colors.

Several innovations in the production of art materials in the 19th century ultimately made it easier for artists to travel. Traditionally, oil colors had been supplied in skin bladders that did not provide effective storage and were cumbersome to carry and use. Paints were expensive, and some pigments, such as vermillion, were especially costly. In 1841, an American artist, John G. Rand, invented a soft-metal collapsible tube that prevented the colors from deteriorating and was easy to transport. At the same time, chemists began to manufacture several pigments artificially. These were becoming more widely available by mid-century.[16]

Itinerant painters either carried their supports, which generally consisted of a fabric canvas, wood panel, or composition board, or acquired them locally. Canvas was the more traditional support, particularly for academically trained painters. Ralph Earl favored full-length portraits and painted on canvases from England and New York. Unable to get canvas wide enough for these paintings in the rural regions of Connecticut and western Massachusetts, Earl used pieced canvases that clearly show one or more seams, rather than scale down his works to fit a single piece of canvas.[17] William Matthew Prior frequently used canvas, but appears to have favored composition board for his less expensive "flat pictures."

The Hartshorns' portraits are on the latter material, however. Zedekiah Belknap used canvas (cat. 27), but also wood panels prepared by scoring the surface diagonally to provide a bite for the paint surface (cat.44). He even used crude bed ticking on at least one occasion.[18] The unidentified artist who painted *Francis Carlisle Babbitt* (cat. 6) apparently resorted to boards from the family's wood shed for painting the child. Another difficulty faced by itinerant painters was that they often needed to move on before paintings were dry and varnished. Thomas Sully (1783-1872) recommended that a painting dry for at least four to five weeks before varnishing.[19] A team of itinerant portrait painters, Richard Jennyes (active 1766-1801) and William Jennyes (active 1793-1807) solved this problem by inscribing the back of a pair of portraits with instructions for their sitters to varnish their own portraits:

> To varnish the Portrait
> Beat the white of an egg to a froth
> and add a small piece of loaf sugar
> and beat it again with two spoonfuls of gin
> Dust the picture
> with a piece of silk and put
> on the varnish with a rag
> To be varnished once in a year [20]

Some portraits were never varnished.

As traveling limners took their skills to nearly every corner of New England, they had to be prepared to work under the conditions at hand, as *The Itinerant Artist* demonstrates. The informality of the setting required the artist to interact with his sitter and her family and listen to the opinions of his unschooled, yet avid, audience. The need to work with speed and efficiency in such chaotic surroundings is evident. Under the circumstances, it must have been all the artist could do to capture a good likeness of his subject. Any hope of imbuing the portrait with the "inner existence" of his sitter would be serendipitous, if not impossible.

THE PORTRAIT AND ITS FUNCTION

THE ROLE OF THE PORTRAIT in American society derived largely from the tradition of the English colonies, where the dominance of portraiture over all other types of painting lasted well into the 19th century. Jonathan Richardson (1665-1745) articulated the function of the portrait in England in his influential 1725 treatise, *An Essay on the Theory of Painting.*

> The Picture of an absent Relation or Friend, helps to keep up those Sentiments which frequently languish by Absence and may be instrumental to maintain, and sometimes augment Friendship, and Paternal, Filial, and Conjugal Love, and Duty. Upon the sight of a Portrait, the character, and master-strokes of the history of the person it represents are apt to flow in upon the mind, and to be the subject of conversation: so that to sit for one's Picture is to have an Abstract of one's life written, and published, and ourselves thus consigned over to Honour or Infamy. [21]

As the function of the portrait changed little over the next hundred years, Richardson's description applies to the early 19th century, as well. Ideally, a portrait signified the entire "history of the person." Rather than capturing one moment in time, the portrait painter tried to convey not only the physical resemblance of the person, but important aspects of an individual's life and achievements. These might include the subject's place within a family, relationship to other family members, social status, professional stature, and domestic endeavors.

In Ezra Woolson's portraits of *Dr. Jesse Kittredge Smith* (cat. 72; pl. 21) and *Permelia Foster Smith,* (cat. 71; pl. 20), painted in Mont Vernon, New Hampshire, in 1842, the artist succeeds in capturing important aspects of the Smiths' lives. Although the full-length format was antiquated by this time, the images are filled with references to their professional and domestic worlds. Dr. Smith is shown with his medical implements, and through the window can be seen several fine carriages arriving at his office. Mrs. Smith is linked to the domestic world of the house, also seen through the window. While both window vignettes are illogical (as the subjects are seated in the house and office), they are effective devices in conveying the spheres in which the sitters functioned.

A characteristic of portraiture in rural New England was the desire for a true likeness, devoid of flattery. Most sitters seemingly wished to be portrayed as they appeared, including signs of age and facial flaws. On the other hand, they wished the artist to convey their social position and affluence. For example, Zedekiah Belknap painted a rather stern portrait of *Elijah Dudley* (cat. 27) in 1829, but returned in 1838 to update his sitter's shirt collar, presumably to reflect the current fashion. On another occasion, Belknap painted a realistic image of a portly subject, *Mr. Jonathan Richardson,* in 1829. In addition to inscribing his sitter's name and age on the back of the wood panel, he also recorded his substantial weight: "The Portrait of Mr. Jonathan Richardson aged 47 yrs. weight. 237./ lb." His weight was presumably a matter of pride to this sitter, who may well have viewed it as a measure of success.[22]

The arrival of a new portrait painter in a prosperous community often prompted a flood of commissions. During a stay in New Bedford, Massachusetts, in 1843, Joseph Whiting Stock noted in his journal, "I have been liberally patronized in this town. ... I have painted to order 37 portraits and 18 miniatures."[23]

On rare occasions, New Englanders commissioned a family portrait, a more expensive form of the genre. It has been noted that family portraits by untrained artists frequently exhibit rather static treatments of the family unit, with all members receiving equal attention, including the children.[24] Robert Peckham's 1835 portrait of *The Doty Family* (cat. 26; pl. 1) of Westminster, Massachusetts, in fact, accords a central prominence to the child, who is proportionately larger than life and stands at head level with his parents. Family portraits often convey filial affection; that of the Doty family also documents their affluence.

A wide variety of forms was available to patrons of portraiture. During the early decades of the 19th century, these included, in addition to conventional oil portraits on canvas or board, less expensive forms, including water-color miniatures on ivory and paper and a variety of profile portraits. Ruth Henshaw Bascom (cat. 11) produced life-size pastel profiles over a period of forty-two years. Her journals indicate that she executed more than one thousand portraits during her career. Although she initially began this work as a pastime, she eventually traveled widely as a professional artist because of financial necessity. Most of her clients were friends and relatives with whom she maintained a continuing relationship. Concerned with obtaining an accurate image, her subjects frequently requested changes to update their profiles. On one occasion, Mrs. Bascom added a pair of spectacles, and on another she "altered the hair of Lydia's picture," years after the original.[25]

Portraits were frequently painted at times of death, particularly the death of a child. The children in many of Stock's posthumous portraits are depicted with symbols of death. For example, the portrait of *Mary and Francis Wilcox* (fig. 11), listed by Stock in his journal in 1845 as the "deceased children of P.F. Wilcox" of Springfield, Massachusetts, shows the children standing surrounded by their favorite toys and a book inscribed "Remember Me." Mary raises her right arm pointing a finger toward heaven.[26] Stock also painted the posthumous portrait of Edward W. Gorham (cat. 39; pl. 12) of Springfield on the day of his death. Stock inscribed the back of the canvas "Feb. 19th 1844/Aged 1 yr. 8 mo. 2 da./ Painted by J.W. Stock" "died." Here he shows the young child busily hammering tacks into a chair, without a specific reference to the fact that this was a posthumous image. Prior *sought* posthumous portrait commissions for children. He claimed that through his conversion in 1841 to the Millerite sect, he had visionary powers that allowed him to see into the spirit world.[27]

Fig. 11. *Joseph Whiting Stock, Mary and Francis Wilcox, 1845, oil on canvas, 48 x 40 (121.9 x 101.6); National Gallery of Art, Washington D.C., gift of Edgar William and Bernice Chrysler Garbisch, 1959.*

Many portrait painters, however, found this practice repugnant, but did posthumous portraits out of compassion for the relatives who desired a memorial. Ruth Henshaw Bascom was occasionally commissioned to take a profile of a child who had just died. In October 1845 she noted in her diary, "At 10 AM went to Mr. J. Stearns by request to try to sketch the features of their deceased daughter—found her in her coffin! but in pitty to her sick + bereaved mother, succeeded in taking the outlines...an only (lovely) daughter aged 14."[28] After completing the portrait of a ten-year-old boy, Charles Blood, who had drowned, the portrait painter, Ethan Allan Greenwood (1779-1856) wrote that "to paint a likeness of a dead person whom I never saw while living is such a job I wish to never undertake. It is disagreeable and uncertain."[29]

From the middle of the 19th-century on, the ideal of the portrait as an image that evoked "the master-strokes of the history of the person," gave way to the new experience of the camera image, which provided an instant and accurate record. Portrait painters were forced to contend with the popularity of this new medium by either embracing it themselves, as did Erastus Salisbury Field and Joseph Whiting Stock, or continuing to compete with it, as Prior did with his rapidly executed and cheap flat paintings. Ultimately, however, most portrait painters lost out to photography.

The young artist George Fuller (1822-1884), in company with his brother Augustus, sensed that the novelty of photography gave it enormous potential as a business and wrote to his father in 1840:

You have heard much (through the papers) of the daguerreotype... Augustus and I went to see the specimens....Now this can be applied to taking miniatures or portraits on the same principles that it takes landscapes. M. Gourand is now fitting up an apparatus for the purpose....The plate (metallic) costs about $1.50, and is easily prepared, but 2 minutes time is required to leave a complete impression on a man's countenance, perfect as nature can make it. He will give me instructions for $10.00 and the apparatus will cost $51.00....This is a new invention, and consequently a great novelty, of which everyone has heard, and has a curiosity to see. It is just what the people in this country like, namely, something new. I think anyone would give $7.00 for their perfect likeness. We could clear ourselves of all expenses in two weeks.[30]

Fuller correctly predicted the enormous appeal of photography for the American public. In comparison to the materials and talent required for painting portraits, this new medium must have seemed less risky.

The rich legacy of portraits executed in rural New England during the first half of the 19th century has provided present-day viewers with a visually enticing and multi-faceted mirror to the past. For a relatively brief period, a segment of American society had its first opportunity to have likenesses taken. This demand encouraged artists with widely ranging levels of skill and ability to flourish. As we have seen in this essay, better understanding of the desires of the patrons, the artists, and the often-unorthodox circumstances in which the portraits were created suggests new ways of looking at the images.

[1] *New England Begins: The Seventeenth Century*, ed. Jonathan L. Fairbanks and Robert F. Trent, 3 vols. (Boston, Museum of Fine Arts, c. 1982), 2:413-479 and Lillian B. Miller, "The Puritan Portrait: Its Function in Old and New England," in *Seventeenth-Century New England* (Boston: The Colonial Society of Massachusetts, 1984), 153-185.

[2] Elizabeth Mankin Kornhauser, *Ralph Earl: Artist-Entrepreneur*, (Ann Arbor, Mich.: University Microfilms, 1989) and Kornhauser, with Richard Bushman, Stephen H. Kornhauser, and Aileen Ribeiro, *Ralph Earl: The Face of the Young Republic*, (New Haven and London: Yale University Press, 1991).

[3] William Dunlap, *History of the Rise and Progress of the Arts of Design in the United States,* ed. Rita Weiss, 3 vols, (1834; reprint, New York: Dover, 1969) 1:195-6.

[4] Grace Adams Lyman, "William M. Prior: The `Painting Garret' Artist," *Antiques* 24 (January, 1934):44.

[5] Dunlap, 2:292.

[6] "Introduction," and "Portraits, Profiles, and Daguerreotypes," in *Itinerancy in New England and New York: The Dublin Seminar For New England Folklife,* ed. Peter Benes (Boston: Boston University, 1986), 5-16, 150-244.

[7] Andrew J. Cosentino, *The Paintings of Charles Bird King, 1785-1862* (Washington: Smithsonian Institution Press, 1977), 38, 41.

[8] *The Paintings and the Journal of Joseph Whiting Stock,* ed. Juliette Tomlinson (Middletown, Conn.: Wesleyan University Press, 1976), 6.

[9] *Journal of Joseph Whiting Stock*, 55-56; see also John Michael Vlach, *Plain Painters: Making Sense of American Folk Art* (Washington and London: Smithsonian Institution Press, 1988), 40-54, discusses this artist in light of his extensive library.

[10] James Guild, "From Turnbridge, Vermont to London England - The Journal of James Guild, Peddler, Tinker, Schoolmaster, Portrait Painter, From 1818-1824," in *Proceedings of the Vermont Historical Society*, 5(1937):268.

[11] Henry T. Tuckerman, *Book of the Artists: American Artist Life* (New York, 1867), 23.

[12] Nina Fletcher Little, "William M. Prior, Traveling Artist, and his In-Laws, the Painting Hamblens," *Antiques* 53 (January 1948):44-48; *American Folk Portraits: Paintings and Drawings from the Abby Aldrich Rockefeller Folk Art Center,* ed. Beatrix T. Rumford (Boston: New York Graphic Society, 1981), 176.

[13] *Maine Inquirer* (Bath), April 5, 1831; *Portrait of Nat Todd* (collection Nina Fletcher Little) in Little, "William M. Prior," *Antiques* 53:45.

[14] *An American Artist, Handbook of Young Artists and Amateurs in Oil Painting* (New York: Wiley & Halsted, 1856), 226, 228.

[15] *The Artist & Tradesman's Guide: Embracing Some of the Leading Facts & Principles of Science, and a Variety of Matter Adapted to the Wants of the Artist, Mechanic, Manufacturere, and Mercantile Community* (New York: Printed by J.C. Johnson, 1829); my thanks to Caroline Sloat who brought this manual to my attention.

[16] Peter Staples et al, *Paint and Painting* (London: The Tate Gallery, 1982), 67-68, 16-17.

[17] Stephen H. Kornhauser, "Ralph Earl's Working Methods and Materials," in Elizabeth Mankin Kornhauser et al, *Ralph Earl: The Face of the Young Republic,* 85-92.

[18] Elizabeth R. Mankin, "Zedekiah Belknap 1781-1858: Itinerant New England Portrait Painter," *Antiques* 110 (November, 1976):1056-1070.

[19] Thomas Sully, *Hints to Young Painters: A Historic Treatise,* intro. by Faber Birren, (1873; repr. New York: Reinhold Pub., 1965), 83.

[20] The inscription appears on the back of *Captain David Judson* and *Grissel Warner Judson,* painted in Huntington, Connecticut, in 1799. The portraits are in the collection of the Chrysler Museum, Norfolk, Virginia.

[21] Jonathan Richardson, *An Essay on the Theory of Painting* (2d ed. 1725; reprint ed. Manston, U.K. 1971), 13-14.

[22] Mankin, *Zedekiah Belknap,* 1059.

[23] *Stock,* ed. Tomlinson, 37

[24] Margaretta M. Lovell, "Reading Eighteenth-Century American Family Portraits," *Winterthur Portfolio* 22(Winter, 1987): 263-264.

[25] Mary Eileen Fouratt, "Ruth Henshaw Bascom, Itinerant Portraitist," *Itinerancy in New England and New York: Annual Proceedings of the Dublin Seminar for New England Folklife,* ed. Benes, (Boston; Boston University, 1986), 200,204.

[26] *Journal of Joseph Whiting Stock,* ed. Tomlinson, 17-18,44.

[27] Lyman, "William M. Prior," 44.

[28] October 15, 1845, Ruth Henshaw Bascom Diaries.

[29] Georgia Brady Bumgardner, "The Early Career of Ethan Allen Greenwood," *Itinerancy,* ed. Benes, 220.

[30] *The Life and Works of George Fuller* (Boston and New York: Houghton-Mifflin, 1886) 14-15, quoted in Grant B. Romer, "'Mirror with a Memory' The Daguerreotype as a Portrait Medium," in *Face to Face: M.W. Hopkins and Noah North* (Lexington, Mass: Museum of our National Heritage), 30.

THE AGE OF
DEMOCRATIC PORTRAITURE
Artisan-Entrepreneurs and the
Rise of Consumer Goods

David Jaffee

THE FEDERAL PERIOD LED TO DRAMATIC CHANGES in the physical and economic context of rural life in New England. It was a new era of production and consumption, of manufacturing and distribution, which had highly visible effects on the furnishings of those who took part in the expansion of the economy. An abundance of colorful commodities, such as shelf clocks, family portraits, and painted chairs, became available to prospering middle-class households throughout the countryside.

Producers began by tapping rural tastes for consumer goods that bespoke status. They then led their customers on to a richer diet of merchandise. In time, rural homes no longer resembled the one depicted by Charles Bird King in *The Itinerant Artist* (pl.11). They came to look, instead, more like that of *Joseph Moore and his Family*, by Erastus Salisbury Field (fig. 12). The *Meet Your Neighbors* exhibit, like other recent studies, takes the position that these consumer goods should not be romanticized as the handiwork of isolated rural craftsmen, who plied their trades until they were pushed aside by the mechanized upheaval of the Industrial Revolution.[1] This essay will trace changes in portraiture by artisans who were aspiring entrepreneurs. These individuals, like those in other economic endeavors, standardized production techniques to satisfy the desires of a growing rural market. New to the economic sphere, they became important agents in the commercialization of the countryside. Through their efforts, portraits were transformed into consumer goods.

I

DURING THE 18TH CENTURY, the limited range and quantity of consumer goods in the homes of inland towns had come from a few sources: urban importers and retailers, country stores, and mostly the rural household itself. As improved transportation and communication began to transform the region's economy, consumer goods played a greater role in the emergence of a market society.[2] Storekeepers prompted the cycle of change by stimulating new business. Their customers became consumers by trading surplus agricultural produce and items they had made within the home for goods from the store. Country merchants, in turn, re-sold the butter and cheese, livestock, brooms, straw braid, palm leaf hats, and other items from their rural communities to urban suppliers as a way of keeping their shelves and bins well stocked.[3]

Fig. 12. Erastus Salisbury Field, Joseph Moore and His Family, 1839, oil on canvas, 82 3/4 x 93 1/4, (210.1 x 238.1). Gift of Maxim Karolik for the M. and M. Karolik Collection of American Paintings, 1815-1865; Courtesy, Museum of Fine Arts, Boston.

These commercial transactions resulted in increased traffic on the roads between the urban areas and the countryside and between rural communities themselves. At the same time, innovative changes in the making of products as diverse as tinware, clocks, and books, were stimulated by alliances between producers and an itinerant sales force. Rural artisans who aspired to entrepreneurship learned that manufacturing and distribution went hand in hand. Those portrait painters who adopted an itinerant lifestyle provide a compelling perspective on the creation of a market society. Their careers reveal that they followed some of the same paths as other artisans in shaping the new economic order of the countryside.

Before the Revolution a small number of portrait makers with academic training had been itinerants. Whether English visitors or travelers between Atlantic port cities, they provided images for both urban and rural leaders. The few rural people who were then able to afford portraits were magistrates and ministers: the established gentry in village society, who found in these unique objects a means to display their personal possessions and social status.[4] Winthrop Chandler (1747-1790), who painted rural family members and town notables, also supplemented his income as a sign, carriage and house painter. Ralph Earl, another painter of rural families, produced portraits and landscape paintings for a Connecticut village elite eager to satisfy its social aspirations. Wealthy clients also patronized other artisans such as clockmakers, who fashioned large and expensive timekeepers for them. Often the most valuable item in a house, a brass clock was a symbol of wealth.

In the decades after the War for Independence, rural artisans in a number of trades expanded their production of commodities and made them affordable to a wider range of rural consumers. Isaiah Thomas, America's foremost publisher during the 18th century, started a new era in the world of printing and bookselling. From his location in Worcester, Massachusetts, a modest county seat of less than 2000 inhabitants, Thomas was the first to exploit the emerging national market for publishing. Following Thomas's promising example, printing offices proliferated in rural New England. From a total of nine in 1760, (virtually all of which were located in Boston, Massachusetts), by 1820, had 120 printing offices scattered throughout the Commonwealth.[5] In another field of endeavor, Simon and Aaron Willard, filled with ideas for manufacturing brass clocks efficiently and in quantity, moved from rural Grafton to Roxbury, Massachusetts, by 1783. In Connecticut, rural entrepreneurs transformed the clock industry by a completely different combination of mechanical and marketing innovations. Experimenting with wooden movements at the beginning of the 19th century, Eli Terry was responsible for a series of developments that made mass production a reality. These innovations were the key to manufacturing several hundred clocks a year.[6]

Portrait painters, like artisans in other trades, were responsible for their own sales and production. Collectively, however, they were able to transform the commodities in which they dealt from scarce and costly luxury items to mass consumer goods.[7] Some portraitists pioneered the rapid (and sometimes mechanically aided) production of likenesses using stylized two-dimensional designs. They standardized their paintings by stock poses, but distinguished their subjects through the inclusion of personal ornaments and possessions. These techniques allowed them to increase productivity and scale their artistic efforts to their customers' pocketbooks. The ingenious and prolific Rufus Porter offered four styles of portraits, ranging from a double "common profile" for twenty cents to an eight-dollar miniature painted on ivory (fig. 13) Side views painted "in full colours" (price torn in handbill; $2.00 in Haverhill advertisement below) and front views ($3.00) were other options. During his career as an itinerant portrait painter, Porter expanded his capacity by constructing the *camera obscura*, a box of mirrors providing "perfect similitude of the objects in view, in full colours, and true perspective." This simple device could be used for tracing onto paper as the basis for a portrait or landscape view. Porter thus reduced the time needed for a portrait to a mere fifteen minutes.

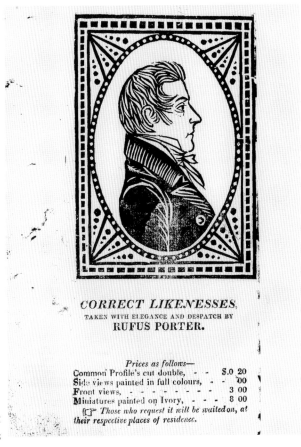

Fig. 13. *"Correct Likenesses, taken with elegance and Despatch by Rufus Porter," 1820-24, sheet: 8 11/16 x 5 1/8 (22 x 13), printed area: 17 1/2 x 3 3/8 (19 x 8.6). Courtesy, American Antiquarian Society.*

With his nephew Joe as his assistant, Porter would stroll into a village, with his brightly decorated camera box mounted on a handcart festooned with flags,[8] and hawk his reasonably priced portraits.

Painting

The subscriber respectfully informs the Ladies and Gentlemen of Haverhill and its vicinity, that he continues to paint correct Likenesses in full Colours for two Dollars at his room at Mr. Brown's tavern, where he will remain two or three Days longer.

(No Likeness, No Pay)

Porter revealed all his techniques in his writings. He described the construction of the *camera obscura* and gave tips for various kinds of painting in *A Select Collection of Approved,*

Genuine, Secret, and Modern Receipts published c. 1824. An article in a series written for the *Scientific American* in 1846 outlined his shortcuts for painting miniatures. His output and income are harder to reconstruct. One author has suggested that a conservative estimate might be at least one thousand portraits: including some 730 likenesses over four years using the *camera obscura*, with his simpler profile silhouettes and miniatures on ivory accounting for the balance. [9]

To be successful, artisans also had to pioneer new distributive networks in conjunction with standardized production. When clockmaker Eli Terry contracted in 1807 with two merchant capitalists who utilized the system of peddling that had been developed for the 18th-century tin-making trade, he could undertake to produce four thousand wooden clock movements in his factory without having to concern himself with selling the clocks individually. In their Brookfield, Massachusetts, printing office, the Merriams adopted two separate strategies that were commonly used by artisans during this era of economic change. One was rural production for an urban market: printing books for city publishers. They also described "driving out 15 to 20 miles to canvass among the country merchants for trade, exchanging books, paper, etc., with merchants in the surrounding towns for such goods as they kept and we could use."[10]

Cumulatively, these artisan-entrepreneurs' innovations in production and distribution resulted in new conceptions of familiar household objects. For example, as the amount and variety of published materials grew, new modes of reading developed. Rural readers' steady diet of sermons and astrological almanacs was supplemented by newspapers and fiction in which the emphasis was on useful knowledge and keeping up with the times. Reading, formerly a conservator of convention, became a force for change.[11] Likewise, when Eli Terry and Seth Thomas improved upon the wooden tall clock movement by producing a viable shelf clock design in 1816, they soon changed the very notion of the clock. It then became an object that lent itself to mass production and distribution. Small (twenty inches tall) and enclosed in a handsome case, it was easily transported and easy to sell. Terry, trained in the 18th-century world in which a clock-maker might produce twenty-five clock movements a year to sell for $25, had succeeded in transforming the industry so that one factory could produce 2500 cased shelf clocks a year at $10.[12] Terry and his contemporaries had developed a flexible system for manufacturing and marketing standardized mass-produced clocks which signified status to a vast rural market across the United States.

Similarly, by the third decade of the 19th-century, as the *Meet Your Neighbors* exhibition suggests, that most exclusive family icon—the portrait—was offered by scores of itinerant artisan-entrepreneurs. Each artist developed his or her own formula for "correct like-nesses": commodities that were consistent with their vernacular training and their patrons' pocketbooks. Rufus Porter still showed the subject's ears in full profile even in his most costly likeness. However, he and numerous other innovative artisans had standardized production with the aid of mechanical inventions and labor-saving techniques and could offer their rural clients as much "art" or "craft" as they were willing to pay for. Porter's mass-produced images mostly catered to the lower ends of the rural market. Other portraitists offered more elaborate likenesses, evincing some urban influence and some knowledge of academic models.

That the artisan-entrepreneurs had successfully created a vast rural marketplace with their production and distribution of a wide range of country-made products is proudly displayed in Joseph Moore's front parlor. Goods that had once been luxuries were among the family's furnishings. The itinerant efforts of Rufus Porter and his artisanal associates promoted a new market culture.

WOULD-BE PORTRAITISTS, encouraged by the desire of rural folks for symbols of a newly achieved gentility came to see the countryside as a vast market for their wares. Writing in 1825 from New York, John Vanderlyn, the academic artist, encouraged his nephew to join the ranks of itinerant portrait makers. He remarked on the buoyant prospects for "moving about through the country" as the painter Ammi Phillips (1787/8-1865) was then doing, filling the apparent demand for "cheap and slight" images. He concluded with a vision of a firm leg up on the social ladder for the supplier of such wares.

> I heard with pleasure that you had made some very clever attempts in portraits where you are and which had given much satisfaction... Were I to begin life again, I should not hesitate to follow this plan, that is, to paint portraits cheap and slight, for the mass of folks can't judge of the merits of a well finished picture... Indeed, moving about through the country as Phillips does...must be an agreeable way of passing ones time... it would besides be the means of introducing a young man to the best society and if he was wise might be the means of establishing himself advantageously in the world.[13]

For many young artisans itinerancy became a stage in the life cycle and an opportunity for upward mobility in the fluid social world of the early republic. The itinerant life provided a way to explore commercial activities and construct new identities.

In post-Revolutionary New England, an itinerant career as a rural portraitist offered geographic, occupational, and social mobility. Itinerancy was also a critical factor in the development and expansion of portraiture in the early 19th century. For some potential consumers, it might provide an introduction to portraiture through a chance encounter with an itinerant artist-entrepreneur. It also gave painters an opportunity to gain training and experience while distributing their products and creating a taste for their services. While Ethan Allen Greenwood studied law in a dilatory way, itinerancy provided a means to a more rewarding career; Chester Harding and Charles Bird King each used a lengthy period of travel as a staging ground for an eventual career as an academic and urban-based artist; and Erastus Salisbury Field was one of a very few artists who spent their entire working lives on the road. To itinerants such as Greenwood, Harding, and Field, traveling was a means of achieving new commercial and cultural roles outside the household economy. Their itinerancy was an effort at self-fashioning that they shared with their rural customers to whom they brought the message as well as the means of social mobility.

Ethan Allen Greenwood's work as an itinerant artist has been viewed as the "prelude to a career as a professional portrait painter in a major American city." As a brash young man of 21, he decided to embark on a painting career. "[I] stretched canvas and brown holland on frames suitable for painting and tried my skill by copying the portrait of Betsey Parker," he wrote in his diary. Four days later he "resolved to have a College education, & returned to Leicester Academy," where he completed his college preparation. He entered Dartmouth College at the age of 22, and while enrolled there, gained experience in portraiture by traveling about to complete commissions. "I began to paint in good earnest," he recalled, "resolved to keep my palette moist and do something every day." He learned to take profiles with a physiognotrace machine, and spent three months studying with the painter Edward Savage, proprietor of the Columbian Gallery in New York. From 1806 until 1813, when he established himself in Boston "to pursue my profession as an artist," he tried a variety of career options—the law, storekeeping, and brick yard ownership—as well as profile taking and portrait painting. In one year-end summary Greenwood wrote:

December 31, 1811: spent this year in painting, travelling, & settling my old affairs. I have painted during the year 66 portraits, some in crayons, & some at reduced prices, on account of the extreme scarcity of money & other causes. As the times are I am content, & feel confident that I have done much better than to have commenced the practice of law.[14]

Chester Harding's discovery of his artistic talent resulted from his travels as a peddler. He moved with his family from New England to western New York in 1806, "then an unbroken wilderness," and sought commercial opportunities outside farming. He and his brother first became involved in chair "turning," but when a local mechanic invented a spinning head and offered Harding the rights to sell the patent in Connecticut, he jumped into his wagon and "was soon out of sight." For the next few years Harding supported himself by plying various rural crafts and occupations along back-country roads. He peddled clocks, established a chair manufactory, and tried tavern keeping. He did a stint as a house painter in Pittsburgh and in slow seasons painted signs, a skill allied with gilding, which he had learned during his days as a chair maker. He next fell in with "one of the Primitive sort," a portrait painter named Nelson,[15] and soon embarked on his journey to becoming one of America's most celebrated portrait painters.

Nelson used a copy of Sir Joshua Reynolds's *Infant Artists* for his sign, incongruously scribing it with the phrase, "Sign, Ornamental and Portrait Painting executed on the shortest notice, with neatness and despatch." Harding later wrote that "painting heads" was the real marvel. He commissioned Nelson to paint likenesses of himself and his wife, "and thought the pictures perfections." Taking home what was in fact a rather crude representation, he pondered by day how a man could produce "such wonders of art" and dreamed by night of commencing such a project himself. Finally, armed with the colors at hand from his own trade, he tried painting his wife's portrait. "The moment I saw the likeness, I became frantic with delight," he recalled. It was like "the discovery of a new sense."[16] Sign painting became odious, and Chester Harding had found his calling.

Enthusiasm and amazement, rather than connoisseurship and criticism, guided this generation of painters and patrons. America's first art critic, John Neal, wrote in 1829 that there existed

a decided disposition for painting in this Country, you can hardly open the door of a best room anywhere, without surprizing or being surprized by the picture of somebody plastered to the wall, and staring at you with both eyes and a bunch of flowers.

Such portraits, "wretched as they are," flourished "in every village of our country," not as luxuries for the rich but as familiar household furnishings, embellishing the homes of ordinary people.[17]

Harding gained proficiency in portraiture by admiring and studying works of art that were available to him in the hinterlands: at first those of his "primitive" mentor in Pittsburgh and then the paintings of a Kentucky native, Matthew Jouett, who had spent time in Gilbert Stuart's Boston studio. He finally went to the Pennsylvania Academy of the Fine Arts in Philadelphia, where he spent time "studying the best pictures, [and] practising at the same time with the brush."[18] Harding thus advanced his career by drawing upon his patrons' desire for cultural goods that emulated metropolitan conventions.

Erastus Salisbury Field was one of the rural portraitists who participated in a two-way transfer of culture between urban and rural settings. His fifty-year career included wide-ranging travel, and his work evolved through several stylistic stages. Aware of their son's talent, Field's parents sent him away in 1824 for a brief period of study with Samuel F.B. Morse (1791-1872) in New York City. Upon his return to Leverett, Mass., he commenced his career by painting portraits of his kin, then took to the road in 1826. Having moved from farm to city and back to the countryside, he ultimately developed his career within the rural idiom and rural system of production.[19]

Field made his way to Hudson, N. Y., where he discovered that the local residents who saw his portraits "think they are good likenesses," and became his patrons. Like many itinerant artists, he relied on family and friends to provide contacts in other communities, as he crossed and re-crossed central New England, completing numerous commissions. Many of his new sitters were related to previous patrons.[20]

At the beginning of the decade of the 1830s, he had painted a portrait of his brother stiffly seated on a hard wooden chair. By the mid-1830s Field had found a means of portraying the rural bourgeoisie in grander poses amid more lavish surroundings. He was satisfying their expectations of elegance at a low price, while relying on stock poses to increase volume. By displaying their personal possessions, Field evolved a formula that simultaneously individualized his sitters and emphasized their status. Field's shorthand technique included stiff frontal poses, square foreshortened hands, and stippled flesh tones. He quickly sketched the general outlines of his male sitters, filling much of the commissioned space with a large dark frock coat. Personal details included fashion accessories and other possessions.

During an 1836 trip to western Massachusetts, Field painted ten members and three generations of the Bassett family of Lee (cats. 12-15, 29), as well as other residents of that community, Pittsfield, and Egremont. The Bassetts' narrow, sloping shoulders contribute to the triangular design of the portraits, which focuses the viewer's attention on the faces. The family patriarchs, Anselm and Nathaniel Bassett (cat. 14), are represented as elderly men. Similarly posed, Anselm's son-in-law, Amos Geer Hulbert, a successful carriage maker (fig. 14), is seated sideways on a grained chair. Hulbert's portrait is distinguished by his ruddy complexion, the book clasped in his left hand, and the books lined up in the left corner. The portrait is strengthened by the dramatic juxtaposition of light and dark tones as well as the brilliantly detailed book bindings.[21] Field's portraits of women reveal a similar process. He found a comfortable pose for his sitters, arranged their hands naturally, added goods to the foreground and details to the background, until his paintings became colorful and decorative displays.

Field's new command of technique and color satisfied his audience's desire to pro-

Fig.14. Erastus Salisbury Field, Amos Geer Hulbert, c. 1836, oil on canvas, 34 1/2 x 29 (87 x 73.66). Private collection.

Fig. 15. The Itinerant Artist, detail of Pl. 11 contrasting the interior with the decoration of the Moore house.

claim their prosperity, for the artist could now surround his subjects with consumer goods. His 1839 portrayal of *Joseph Moore and His Family* (fig. 12) is the traveling portrait maker's celebration of the consumption of mass-produced objects. The parlor's green shutters are closed to protect the curtains and carpet from sunlight. Within the room, the patterns of the painted chairs and veneered mirror and table catch the light. Faces and figures do not dominate; the viewer's eye jumps from the black-and-white-clad subjects to the numerous, colorful possessions. (In contrast, a retrospective painting, Charles Bird King's *The Itinerant Artist* [c. 1830], offers a glimpse into an earlier period of rural consumerism (fig.15). The family is clustered in the dark monochromatic kitchen, with its wooden floor, where the most abundant goods are woodenware and ceramics. Through a doorway, a bedroom is seen with a bed and somewhat old-fashioned chairs. The portrait will take its place among the first consumer goods to enter this particular household.)

Usually working within the constraints of time and the price his patrons would pay, the rural portrait-maker aimed at simplicity and even stark linearity, which accompanied broad expanses of color and texture. The Moores chose to be portrayed in their parlor amidst fashionable furnishings that arrest our attention with their exuberant colors. The image of the Moore family shows how residents of the emerging commercial villages of New England—painter and patron—constructed new middle class identities. But in 1839, the very same year in which Field painted this icon of middle class life, the daguerreotypist's art began to replace the "correct likeness" with "perfect likenesses," and a new era dawned for rural image-makers.

IV

THE CRITICAL ROLE OF ITINERANT PORTRAITISTS in the popularization of the photograph—the "perfect likeness"— demonstrates the success of the model for distribution. Mobile artisan/artists had already promoted entrepreneurial activity in the countryside to a well-developed audience of consumers. With the development of standardized family pictures, itinerant portraitists' efforts had introduced visions of urban elegance to village life. The mechanical process of photography made even greater numbers of cheap images available to rural residents.

The commercial possibilities of the daguerreotype were recognized immediately by shrewd portraitists, who headed out to the countryside. The painter George Fuller wrote to his father from Boston in April of 1840 that he proposed to purchase a camera and take lessons: "But two minutes' time is required to leave a complete impression of a man's countenance, perfect as nature can make it." Urban figures trained multitudes of practitioners and rural people proved to be a receptive market for straightforward photographs. L.C. Champney wrote in 1843 from Bennington, Vermont, to his teacher, A.S. Southworth, owner of an elegant Boston establishment:

> I think I shall stay up this way for the present. They all say that my pictures are the best that they ever saw. I have tride the light as you proposed, but they do not like the dark on one side of the face, and I cant sell a picture that where one side of the face is darker than the other, altho it seems to stand out better and look richer. [22]

Itinerant operators were quick to offer their rural customers a variation of the elegance of urban studios by fitting up wagons as "Daguerreotype Saloons." Every city and town had at least one gallery, according to the first historian of the daguerreotype, and "itinerant daguerreotypists traveled to remote backwoods and frontier areas in their horse-drawn 'saloons,' or floated down the rivers in houseboats." From Louisville, Kentucky, came the report in 1855: "There is not a place of one hundred inhabitants in any of the Southern or Western states that have not been visited by from one to any number of itinerants." Within a decade, daguerreotyping was recognized as an industry, and itinerant operators or "Daguerrean Artists" were critical figures in building a market for family likenesses. T.S. Arthur, the popular author, wrote in 1848 for the readers of *Godey's Lady's Book* that every individual could own a likeness of an ancestor, every home could be a daguerrean gallery, and every "operator" could be an artist.

> A few years ago it was not every man who could afford a likeness of himself, his wife or his children; these were luxuries known only to those who had money to spare; now it is hard to find the man who has not gone through the "operators" hands from once to half-a-dozen times, or who has not the shadowy faces of his wife and children done up in purple morocco and velvet, together or singly, among his household treasures.

It was reported that 403,626 daguerreotypes had been taken in Massachusets during 1855, the work of 134 "Daguerreotype Artists." In 1860 the U.S. Census reported 3,154 photographers.[23]

The introduction of fully mechanized portraiture also altered other relationships. The rage for portraits led many itinerant painters into attempts to incorporate the new technology. Some, such as Joseph Whiting Stock and John Toole, simply offered daguerreotypes at their studios in addition to likenesses in oil. Others, like Erastus Field, initially tried to imitate the photograph's appeal and attempted a more realistic image. But the cheaper price and greater verisimilitude of the photograph put the ordinary portrait maker at a severe disadvantage. A broadside from western Massachusetts in 1841 argued that,

> The precise expression of the face at the time of setting in its minutest features will be at once and forever fixed; engraved as it were by the sunbeams, and as the operation

seldom exceeds a minute, and is often finished in a few seconds, it is evident that the expression of the face may be fixed in the picture which are too fleeting to be caught by the painter. By such flashes of the soul we remember our friends, and these cannot appear on the canvass.[24]

A rural portraitist such as Robert Peckham met the challenge of photography by adapting his pictorial style for the emerging industrial elite of Worcester County, Massachusetts. Peckham, a lifelong resident of Westminster, Massachusetts, had studied briefly with Ethan Allen Greenwood in 1809. Beginning as a somewhat provincial decorative painter, he soon became an accomplished artist. By the 1830s Peckham's standard portrait format indicated his familiarity with 19th-century academic traditions. He knew how to draw, and he concentrated on realistic modeling through the use of light and shadow. In 1842 he painted the wedding portraits of Newton and Sarah Puffer Hubbard of Brimfield, Massachusetts (cats. 46, 47). Like his other depictions of women, Sarah Hubbard's portrait is almost exclusively in black and white, with the exception of the flesh tones, brown hair, and reddish brown background. The artist successfully contrasts the somber clothing and background with the subject's decorated white collar and softly modeled facial features, an effect which draws the viewer's eye to the face.[25]

Fig. 16. Robert Peckham, Rosa Heywood, c. 1840, oil on canvas, 44 1/4 x 29 1/4 (112 x 74.3). Abby Aldrich Rockefeller Folk Art Center, Colonial Williamsburg Foundation.

The Doty Family of 1835 (cat. 26; pl. 1) varies from Peckham's standard product. In this image of a prosperous Westminster family, headed by Timothy Doty, a merchant and town officer, color and decorative detail stand out more than usual, with the red book and curtains, sofa, pocket watch, jewelled earrings and silver buckle. As in Field's Moore Family, the artist celebrates a rural family's arrival into affluence, surrounded by their plentiful possessions. The colorful and abundant appointments of these households contrasts dramatically with the old-fashioned and dimly lit interior of King's Itinerant Artist.

This era of democratic portraiture ultimately ended with the transformation of image-making through photographic reproduction. Oil portraits returned to their status as elite objects. The new photographic images became the means of preserving likenesses. Thus, in the 1840s, Peckham's portraiture recorded a new image of affluent childhood showing the children of newly wealthy manufacturers. In his portrait of Rosa Heywood (1840), the only child of chair manufacturer Walter Heywood, Peckham gave no hint of the Heywoods's rural past (figs. 16, 17). Heywood was one of a group of entrepreneurs who had transformed chair-making in central Massachusetts from a task largely performed by farmers in the winter months to a factory-based industry, waterpower, and new modes of business organization. His child's portrait is evidence that he enjoyed the trappings of success. [26]

V

EARLY 19TH-CENTURY PORTRAITS, like other standardized and colorful country wares—chairs, clocks, and books—were made by rural craftsmen in an era of decentralized production. Country artisans and merchants moved beyond merely carrying goods into distant corners of rural New England; they helped introduce people to the business of acquiring goods. And producer and consumer shared in the activity of self-fashioning through the purchase of commodities.

The importance of rural artisan-entrepreneurs in the economic life of New England was declining by mid-century. Ironically, their success in creating a vast marketplace for cheap consumer goods brought an end to their way of doing business. The system of decentralized production and distribution was giving way to the much larger-scale structures of urban manufacturing and marketing.[27] Some rural manufacturers, like the Merriams or the Heywood Brothers were able to adapt to large-scale production. Many others would be displaced. The sumptuous interior of the Heywood house as painted by Robert Peckham indicates wealth on a level far above that of mere prosperity, and suggests that the age of democratic portraiture was coming to an end.

Fig. 17. Victorian Side Chair, c. 1860, Heywood Brothers and Co., H: 31, W:17, D:14 1/2. Courtesy, Gardner Museum. By mid-century the Heywood Brothers had standardized the production of the side chair with its lathe-turned legs and rails and elaborate free-hand painted scene. The glimpse of the house in the portrait and the factory-made chair indicate that the Heywoods participated in the process of democratization as both producers and consumers.

[1] On the changing rural world, see Christopher Clark, *The Rise of Rural Capitalism* (Ithaca: Cornell University Press, 1990); *The Countryside in the Age of Capitalist Transformation: Essays in the Social History of Rural America*, Steven Hahn and Jonathan Prude, eds., (Chapel Hill: University of North Carolina Press, 1985).

On new modes of rural production and consumption, see Jack Larkin, "The Merriams of Brookfield: Printing in the Economy and Culture of Rural Massachusetts in the Early 19th Century," Proceedings of the American Antiquarian Society 96 (1986):39-73; Elisabeth D. Garrett, *At Home: The*

American Family, 1750-1870 (New York: Harry N. Abrams, 1990).

[2] On rural transformation, see the review essays by Gregory Nobles, "Capitalism in the Countryside: The Transformation of Rural Society in the United States," *Radical History Review* 41 (Spring 1988):168-177; Allan Kulikoff, "The Transition to Capitalism in Rural America," *William and Mary Quarterly* 46 (January 1989):120-144.

[3] See Jack Larkin, "Massachusetts Enters the Marketplace, 1790-1860: An Interpretation of Recent Work in Social History," *A Guide to the History of Massachusetts*, Martin

Kaufman, John W. Ifkovic, and Joseph Carvalho III (Westport, Conn: Greenwood Press, 1988); Joseph Wood, "Elaboration of a Settlement System—The New England Village in the Federal Period," *Journal of Historical Geography* 10 (Winter 1984):331-356; Andrew Baker and Holly Izard Paterson, "Farmers' Adaptations to Markets in Early-Nineteenth-Century Massachusetts," *The Farm: Annual Proceedings of the Dublin Seminar for New England Folklife*, 1986, ed. Peter Benes, (Boston: Boston University, 1988).

[4] Winthrop Chandler: Nina Fletcher Little, "Winthrop Chandler," *American Folk Painters of Three Centuries*, ed. Jean Lipman and Tom Armstrong (New York: Hudson Hills Press, 1980), 26-34; Nina Little, "Winthrop Chandler," *Art in America* 35 (1947) entire issue. Ralph Earl: Laurence B. Goodrich, *Ralph Earl: Recorder for an Era* (Albany: State University of N.Y., 1967); Elizabeth Kornhauser, "Ralph Earl as an Itinerant Artist: Patterns of Patronage," *Itinerancy in New England and New York: Annual Proceedings of the Dublin Seminar for New England Folklife*, ed. Peter Benes (Boston: Boston University, 1986), 172-189.

[5] See Isaiah Thomas, *The History of Printing in America*, 2 vols (Worcester, Mass.: Isaiah Thomas, 1810); Richard D. Brown, "The Emergence of Urban Society in Rural Massachusetts, 1760-1820," *Journal of American History* 61 (1971):43-44.

[6] Henry Terry, *American Clock Making, its early history and present extent of the business* (Waterbury, Conn.: Henry Terry, 1870), 4-6; John Joseph Murphy, "Entrepreneurship in the Establishment of the American Clock Industry, *Journal of Economic History* 24(1966):168-186; Chris Bailey, *Two Hundred Years of American Clocks and Watches* (Englewood Cliffs, N.J.: Prentice Hall, 1975).

[7] See David Jaffee, "One of the Primitive Sort: Portrait Painters of the Rural North, 1760-1860," in Hahn and Prude; John Michael Vlach, *Plain Painters: Making Sense of American Folk Art* (Washington: Smithsonian Institution Press, 1988).

[8] Jean Lipman, *Rufus Porter Rediscovered: Artist, Inventor, Journalist 1792-1884* ([1968] New York: Clarkson Potter, 1980); "Rufus Porter, Founder of the Scientific American," *Scientific American* (Sept. 6, 1884).

[9] Advertisement from *Haverhill* (Mass.) *Gazette*, March 31, 1821, reprinted in Lipman, *Rufus Porter*, 5, 63-88; *American Folk Portraits: Paintings and Drawings from the Abby Aldrich Rockefeller Folk Art Center*, ed. Beatrix Rumford (Boston: Little, Brown, 1981), 169-172.

[10] Larkin, "The Merriams of Brookfield," 39-72.

[11] See Cathy N. Davidson, *Revolution and the Word: The Rise of the Novel in America* (New York: Oxford University Press, 1986); David D. Hall, "Introduction: The Uses of Literacy in New England, 1600-1850," *Printing and Society in Early America*, ed. William L. Joyce, David D. Hall, Richard D. Brown, and John B. Hench (Worcester: American Antiquarian Society, 1983).

[12] John Joseph Murphy, "The Establishment of the American Clock Industry: A Study in Entrepreneurial History," (Ph.D. Dissertation, Yale University, 1961), 56.

[13] John Vanderlyn to John Vanderlyn, Jr., September 9,

1825, in Barbara C. Holdridge and Lawrence B. Holdridge, *Ammi Phillips: Portrait Painter, 1788-1865* (New York: Museum of American Folk Art, 1968), 14.

[14] Georgia B. Bumgardner, "The Early Career of Ethan Allen Greenwood," *Itinerancy*, ed. Benes, 213-225.

[15] Chester Harding, *A Sketch of Chester Harding, Artist* (Cambridge, Mass.: Riverside Press, 1890), 5, 10, 17-18; Leah Lipton, *A Truthful Likeness: Chester Harding and His Portraits* (Washington: National Portrait Gallery, 1985).

[16] Harding, *Sketch*, 18-20.

[17] John Neal, "American Painters and Painting," *The Yankee: and Boston Literary Gazette* I (1829):45.

[18] Harding, *Sketch*, 24-25; Lipton, *Truthful Likeness*.

[19] See Mary Black, *Erastus Salisbury Field: 1805-1900* (Springfield, Mass.: Museum of Fine Arts, 1984); *American Folk Portraits*, ed. Rumford, 93-99.

[20] Black, *Erastus Salisbury Field*, 14, 20-21.

[21] *American Folk Portraits*, ed. Rumford, 93-99; Black, *Erastus Salisbury Field*, 20.

[22] *George Fuller: His Life and Works*, ed. Josiah B. Millet (Boston: Houghton, Mifflin 1886), 14; Champney to Southworth, quoted in Beaumont Newhall, *The Daguerreotype in America* ([1961], New York: Drell, Sloan and Pierce, 1976) 69-70. See Robert Taft, *Photography and the American Scene*, 1964, New York: Dover Publications, 1964); Richard Rudishill, *Mirror Image: The Influence of the Daguerreotype on American Society* (Albuquerque: University of New Mexico Press, 1981).

[23] Newhall, *Daguerreotype*, 32-34; Fitzgibbon quoted in Newhall, 37; T.S. Arthur, "American Characteristics: The Daguerreotypist," *Godey's Lady's Book* 38(1849):352-55.

[24] Anson and E.H. Clark Broadside, West Stockbridge, June 12, 1841, reproduced in Edna Bailey Garnett, *West Stockbridge, Massachusetts, 1774-1974* (Great Barrington, MA: Berkshire Courier, 1976), 109. *The Paintings and the Journal of Joseph Whiting Stock*, ed. Juliette Tomlinson (Middletown, Conn.: Wesleyan University Press, 1976); William B. O'Neal, *Primitive into Painter: Life and Letters of John Toole* (Charlottesville, Va.: University Press of Virginia, 1960), 26.

[25] See Dale T. Johnson, "Deacon Robert Peckham: Delineator of the 'Human Face Divine'," *American Art Journal* 11(January 1979):27-36; Laura C. Luckey, "The Portraits of Robert Peckham, *Antiques* 134(September 1988):552-7; Paul D'Ambrosio and Charlotte M. Emans, *Folk Art's Many Faces* (Cooperstown, N.Y.: New York Historical Association, 1987), 124-5.

[26] *A Completed Century 1826-1926: The Story of the Heywood-Wakefield Company* (Boston: Heywood-Wakefield Co., 1926); Esther G. Moore, *History of Gardner, Massachusetts, 1785-1967* (Gardner, 1967).

[27] Alfred D. Chandler, *The Visible Hand: The Managerial Revolution in American Business* (Cambridge MA: Harvard University Press, 1977); Glenn Porter and Harold C. Livesay, *Merchants and Manufacturers: Studies in the Changing Structure of Nineteenth Century Marketing* (Baltimore: Johns Hopkins University Press, 1971).

COLOR PLATES

Pl.1. The Doty Family, Robert Peckham, Forbush Memorial Library, Westminster, Massachusetts. (cat. 26)

Pl. 2. Mrs. Nancy Lawson, William Matthew Prior, Shelburne
Museum. Shelburne, Vermont, Photograph by Ken Burris. (cat. 53)

Pl. 3. Mr. William Lawson, William Matthew Prior, Shelburne
Museum, Shelburne, Vermont, Photograph by Ken Burris. (cat. 54)

Pl. 4. The Artist as a Young Man: A Self-Portrait, William Matthew Prior, Signed on the back: Wm. Matthew Prior, Painter, Portland, Maine Oct. 12, 1825, oil on canvas, 27 x 31 (68.6 x 78.8), Hirschl and Adler Galleries, Inc, New York City.

Pl. 5. Dolly Floyd Wiley, Erastus Salisbury Field, Museum of Fine Arts, Springfield, Massachusetts. (cat. 78)

Pl. 6. Bethiah Bassett, Erastus Salisbury Field, Smith College Museum of Art, Northampton, Massachusetts. (cat. 14)

Pl. 7. Nathaniel Bassett, Erastus Salisbury Field, Smith College Museum of Art, Northampton, Massachusetts. (cat. 15)

Pl. 8. Elizabeth Stone Denny, Augustus Fuller,
Worcester Historical Museum. (cat. 24)

Pl. 9. Edwards Whipple Denny, Augustus Fuller,
Worcester Historical Museum. (cat. 25)

Pl. 10. Fanny Negus Fuller and her twin sons, Francis Benjamin and John Emery, Augustus Fuller, Deerfield Academy, (cat. 33)

Pl. 11. The Itinerant Artist,
Charles Bird King (1785-1862),
oil on canvas, ca. 1850,
44 3/4 x 57 (111.2 x 144.8),
New York State Historical Association,
Cooperstown.

Pl. 12. Edward W. Gorham, Joseph Whiting Stock, New York State Historical Association, Cooperstown. (cat. 39)

Pl. 13. Sarah Shedd, Sanford Mason, private collection.(cat. 68)

Pl. 14. Philena Allbee Adams, Aaron Dean Fletcher,
Old Sturbridge Village. (cat. 2)

Pl. 15. Mark White Adams, Aaron Dean Fletcher,
Old Sturbridge Village (cat. 3)

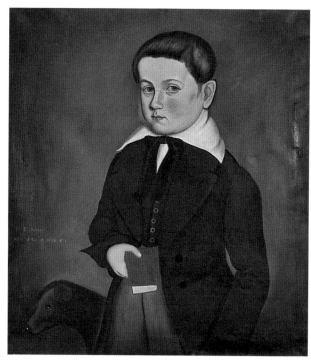

Pl. 16. Luthera A. Adams, Aaron Dean Fletcher,
Old Sturbridge Village. (cat. 4)

Pl. 17. Hiram Ebenezer Adams, Aaron Dean Fletcher,
Old Sturbridge Village. (cat. 5)

Pl. 18. Mrs. Moses Green, Ruth Henshaw Bascom,
Old Sturbridge Village. (cat. 40)

Pl. 19. Moses Green, Ruth Henshaw Bascom,
Old Sturbridge Village. (cat. 41)

Pl. 20. Permelia Foster Smith, Ezra Woolson, Old Sturbridge Village. (cat. 71)

Pl. 21. Jesse Kittredge Smith, Ezra Woolson, Old Sturbridge Village. (cat. 72)

Pl. 22. Harriet Evelith Kilner, William Fisk Ainsworth,
Old Sturbridge Village. (cat. 49)

Pl. 23. Frederick Kilner, William Fisk Ainsworth,
Old Sturbridge Village. (cat. 50)

Pl. 24. Tirzah Waite Bowdoin, David Waite Bowdoin,
Old Sturbridge Village. (cat. 17)

Pl 25. James Bowdoin, David Waite Bowdoin,
Old Sturbridge Village. (cat. 18)

CATALOG
OF THE
EXHIBITION

Jessica F. Nicoll

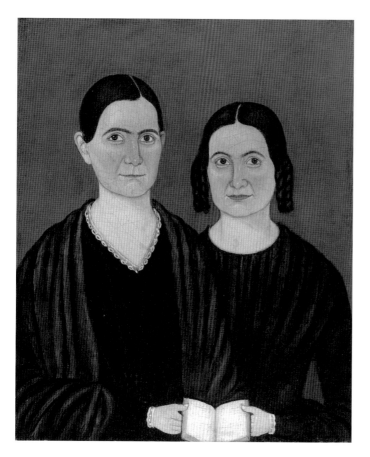

1.
HANNAH THURSTON ADAMS
(1809-1872)
MARY AGNES ADAMS (1812-1890)
Unknown Artist
Manchester, N.H., c. 1845
Oil on canvas
17 1/2 x 14 3/4 (44.5 x 37.5)
Private Collection

THIS SMALL PAINTING makes a surprisingly forceful statement with its depiction of two sisters standing shoulder to shoulder. Hannah and Mary Adams are jointly holding a book, which may represent a ledger for their prospering Manchester, N.H., millinery and tailoring business. They took great pride in their success and expressed the independence it afforded them by commissioning their own portrait. This painting tangibly represents "The Manchester Sisterhood," as Hannah and Mary described their partnership.[1]

The first and third of Elizabeth and Edmund

Adams's eight children, Hannah and Mary were born and raised on a farm in "Cowbell Corner," a section of North Salem, N.H.[2] Their early education was in the Salem district schools. Hannah later attended Atkinson Academy while Mary was enrolled for two years at Adams Female Academy (named for an uncle whose bequest created the school).[3] There, Mary studied under Zilpah Grant and Mary Lyon, who founded Mount Holyoke Seminary in 1837. Grant and Lyon's strong views on female education and the potential of women may well have influenced Mary's lifelong love of learning and her determined independence.

The Adams's farm could not support the whole family, so as the older children reached maturity, each sought a trade. In 1829, Hannah was certified to teach school, which she did until illness forced her into a prolonged convalescence in 1832. Meanwhile, Mary served an apprenticeship in Nashua with a tailor, Patrick Hickey. She was clear in her purpose, as shown by her request to be taught "the whole of the tailoring trade."[4] By this she meant learning the system for cutting tailored garments, such as coats, so that when her apprenticeship ended she could establish her own business. Aware that knowledge of cutting would liberate her from the drudgery of working long hours for poor pay in another tailor's shop, Mary struggled throughout her apprenticeship to persuade Hickey to reveal the secrets of his craft.

When Hannah had fully recovered from her illness she joined Mary in Nashua to learn millinery and dress-making as an apprentice to Miss Brown. One of four young women in the shop, she must have shown ability, for when her apprenticeship concluded in October 1834, Miss Brown kept her on for $1.00 a week.[5] Mary, the nascent businesswoman, urged Hannah to start her own shop, but Hannah was reluctant, explaining to her parents: "I think I shall not like it...it comes rather odd to me to wait upon customers & sell our fancy work and stuff."[6]

Four years later Hannah had overcome these qualms. She and Mary established their millinery and tailoring business in Manchester on the advice of their younger sister Eliza, a textile mill operative.[7] Initially, they worked for another city tailor but before long they began "to be hurried with work" of their own.[8] The business accounts for 1839 show the sisters employed making coats, pants, vests, and other garments traditionally custom-made by tailors. Within eighteen months from the start of the business, Hannah and Mary had earned money and confidence enough in Manchester to build the house in which they resided for the remainder of their lives.[9]

When the volume of work was too great for Hannah and Mary, they employed their sisters, Eliza and Margaret. Usually no more than three sisters were in Manchester, so that a fourth could help their parents at home. This duty frequently fell to Margaret, the youngest, but all of the sisters shared this responsibility. Although the senior Adams's could not afford to support their daughters, this did not prevent Mrs. Adams from chiding Hannah and Mary that it would be more seemly for them "to stay at home and help their mother until they ... married." This charge prompted Hannah and Mary to speak out in self defense:

> My dear Mother we are not wanting in affection for you, but do you can you as one so kind & tender hearted to your children, believe this dreadful doctrine that your daughters were born slaves to serve you until they are married & afterwards it may be to serve drunken husbands — It were better that they had never been born than to be born slaves — But Mother you do not believe it, I feel that you do not believe it. Are we not as good & free to act for ourselves as your sons? If we are not pray tell us for we are yet to learn that daughters of freeborn citizens are not as free as sons according to the laws of our country.[10]

The circumstances of Hannah and Mary Adams's lives were not substantially different from most of their generation. They were born to a rural farm family at a time when an economic shift away from agriculture and toward industry drew young men and women from the countryside to manufacturing centers. However, unlike most women, for whom work outside the home was only an interlude before marriage, Hannah and Mary approached their trades like men, shaping them into lifelong occupations. Not swept along by the events of their lives, they consciously chose their roles.

The Adams sisters were among the single women, less than ten percent of New England's population in the 1840s, who sought fulfillment through work,

community service, and education.[11] Three years after establishing themselves in Manchester, Hannah wrote: "we are as happy as pigs in the clover, nothing to do but work & of that we are overrun—after we lay our work aside we have plenty of intellectual enjoyment, books & papers, meetings & lectures."[12] Both sisters' letters and Mary's diary for 1846-1852 show their awareness of world events and abound with details of lectures attended, books read, and social causes championed. Empowered by their business and confident in their abilities, Hannah and Mary Adams exploited their spinsterhood for the freedom it permitted to cultivate their selves.

[1] The Adams sisters bound their letters and "The Manchester Sisterhood" is one of their volumes. Their correspondence, diaries, and business accounts are in a private collection and are used with permission.

[2] Jo Anne Preston, "Learning a Trade in Industrializing New England: The Expedition of Hannah and Mary Adams to Nashua, N.H., 1833-1834," *Historical New Hampshire*, 39 (Spring/Summer 1984): 25-26.

[3] Preston, "Learning a Trade," 25-26; *Catalogue of the Adams Female Academy, 1824, 1825, 1826* (Concord, 1827), 5, 9.

[4] Mary Adams to Thomas Brenden, 18 December 1832.

[5] Hannah Adams to Aunt Margaret Karr, 14 September 1834. No further identification of Miss Brown has been possible.

[6] Hannah Adams to her family, 3 August 1834.

[7] Eliza Adams to Margaret Adams, 20 December 1837.

[8] Mary or Hannah Adams to Margaret Adams, 9 September 1838.

[9] Hannah Adams to Eliza Adams, 10 May 1839.

[10] Hannah and Mary Adams to Elizabeth Karr Adams, 23 March 1842.

[11] Lee Virginia Chambers-Schiller, *Liberty, A Better Husband* (New Haven and London: Yale University Press, 1984), 7.

[12] Hannah Adams to Edmund and Elizabeth Adams, 14 November 1841.

2.
PHILENA ALLBEE ADAMS
(1795-1866)
Aaron Dean Fletcher
(1817-1902)
Rockingham, Vt., 1837
Oil on canvas
26 3/4 x 23 5/8 (68 x 60)
Inscribed lower right:
P. ADAMS/BORN MARCH 29
1795 AE 42
Old Sturbridge Village
Plate 14

Cat. 2

From left to right:
Cats. 3, 4, and 5

3.
MARK WHITE ADAMS (1790-1858)
Aaron Dean Fletcher (1817-1902)
Rockingham, Vt., 1837
Oil on canvas
27 3/8 x 24 1/4 (69.5 x 61.6)
Inscribed lower left: *M W ADAMS./BORN MAY 22, 1790.*
AE 47
Old Sturbridge Village
Plate 15

4.
LUTHERA ADAMS (1825-1890)
Aaron Dean Fletcher (1817-1902)
Rockingham, Vt., 1837
Oil on canvas
26 1/8 x 23 1/8 (66.4 x 58.8)
Inscribed lower right: *L A ADAMS/*
BORN MAY 4 1825 AE 12
Old Sturbridge Village
Plate 16

5.
HIRAM EBENEZER ADAMS (1828-1904)
Aaron Dean Fletcher (1817-1902)
Rockingham, Vt., 1837
Oil on canvas
29 1/8 x 26 1/2 (74 x 67.3)
Inscribed lower left: *H E ADAMS/ BORN JULY 4 1828*
AE 9
Old Sturbridge Village
Plate 17

PORTRAITS WERE LESS LIKELY TO BE HUNG in New England's farm dwellings than on the walls of merchants' and artisans' houses in commercial center villages. Only in the homes of the most substantial farmers, like the prosperous James Bowdoin (cat. 18)

or the politically influential Elihu Hoyt (cat. 45), were painted representations of their residents found. For upwardly mobile farmers, the commissioning and ownership of portraits was a process of self-definition, signifying position and power. When Mark Adams, an "extensive farmer," invested in these portraits of his family they were expressions of social attainments as well as aspirations.[1]

The collective likenesses of Mark, Philena, Luthera, and Hiram represent the Adams family group as it existed in 1837.[2] The four portraits show each family member carefully dressed in stylish outfits that distance them from the manual labor of the farm and place them amidst the parlor gentility of the center village. Beyond articulating social identity, these images clearly define individual roles and responsibilities. In each portrait the held objects, which at first may appear to be insignificant items introduced to still a sitter's fidgety hands, are important symbols of identity.

As a farmer, Mark Adams's decision to be depicted holding his wallet is particularly intriguing. In the early 19th-century many farmers still operated largely within a barter economy, so Adams's wallet distinguishes him as someone engaged in cash transactions. The land records for Rockingham show Adams investing heavily in land between 1825 and 1858. During that time he amassed holdings of over 1200 acres, primarily farm lands.[3] In his pastures Adams raised sheep and cattle for sale in the urban livestock markets.[4] When he drove his animals to the city, cash was essential for paying expenses and for conducting business. Adams's firm grasp on his wallet calls to mind drovers' accounts expressing fear of becoming targets for robbers.

The wallet identifies Mark Adams as the family member who engaged in exchange with the outside world. In contrast, Philena Adams holds her knitting, an emblem of nurture and of her domestic responsibilities. This distinction of gender roles sums up the notion of separate spheres articulated in early 19th-century advice literature. A wife's employment was:

> To attend to the nursing and early instruction of children, and rear a healthy progeny in the ways of piety and usefulness — to preside over the family and regulate the income allotted to its maintenance; to make home the sweet refuge of a husband fatigued by intercourse with the jarring world.[5]

Depicted in her neat clothing, while knitting a stocking and gazing with tired eyes, Philena's dedication to these household duties is easy to imagine.

The portraits of Luthera and Hiram offer evidence of their careful upbringing. Luthera's clothing is an important gauge of her knowledge of fashion and understanding of good taste. Her white dress may demonstrate her developing skill with a needle, but she does not hold a traditional icon of female accomplishment, such as sewing. Rather, she clasps a book, showing that she can read and implying that she is attending school. At a time when women's educational opportunities were increasing and, as teachers and writers, women were expanding their role in society, this small volume may allude to increased possibilities for Luthera's adult life.

Hiram posed with his pet dog, which family tradition recalls was named "Dog." This animal likely played a role on the Adams farm, but here it is shown as a patient, domesticated companion. Pet-keeping became increasingly common during the 19th-century, as it was deemed beneficial for teaching children stewardship of dependent beings. Like his sister, Hiram is shown with a book. At this age he was probably attending a district school, but by 1844 he was enrolled at an academy in neighboring Saxtons River.[6] That his parents sent Hiram to private school is a testament to their aspirations for their son. While Hiram did not go into one of the learned professions, neither did he become a farmer. Early in adulthood he worked briefly as a carpenter until becoming a merchant, later specializing in jewelry.[7]

These carefully conceived likenesses are characteristic of Aaron Dean Fletcher's (cats. 62, 63, 64) style; the inscriptions, listing sitter's name and age, are like those on his other signed paintings. Beginning around 1835, the artist traveled the countryside near his home in Springfield, Vt., painting portraits of its residents until about 1840, when he moved on to New York state. In these paintings of a farm family, he employed the same imagery of middle-class respectability seen in his portraits of the community's merchants, ministers, and craftsmen.[8]

[1] Lyman Simpson Hayes, *History of the Town of Rockingham, Vt. Including Bellows Falls* (1907), 569.
[2] The Adamses also had a twenty year old son, Lucius, who had left home by 1837. Their two other children, Hiram Hunt and Mary Philena, had died before these portraits were painted; Hayes, *History*, 569.
[3] Thanks to Sally Fuller for checking Mark Adams's land transactions at the Bellows Falls Registry of Deeds.
[4] Hayes, *History*, 569.
[5] Maria E. Rundell, *A New System of Domestic Cookery Formed Upon Principles of Economy* (New York, 1815), iii.
[6] *Catalogue of Officers, Instructors and Students of Saxtons River Academy, Rockingham, Vt.* (Bellows Falls, 1844) cited in Virginia M. Burdick and Nancy C. Muller, "Aaron Dean Fletcher, portrait painter", *Antiques*, 115 (January 1979): 184.
[7] Hayes, *History*, 569-570; Lillian Baker Carlisle, *Vermont Clock and Watchmakers, Silversmiths and Jewelers, 1778-1878* (Burlington, 1970), 41-42.
[8] Burdick and Muller, "Aaron Dean Fletcher", 184-193.

6.

FRANCIS CARLISLE BABBITT

(1836-1906)
Unknown Artist
Syracuse, N.Y., c. 1839
Oil on panel
40 1/2 x 18 1/8 (102.9 x 46)
Shelburne Museum, Shelburne, Vt.

THREE-YEAR-OLD Francis Babbitt is vividly dressed in a green surtout, yellow vest, blue pantaloons, and a white shirt with a black bow. Late in life, the subject remembered being reluctant to stop playing to pose for this likeness dressed in his "Sunday best." The portrait was the result of a conflict between the artist and the subject's parents, Lucius and Sophronia Babbitt, over the painter's inability to pay for his room and board in the Babbitt household. In negotiating to paint the portrait in lieu of payment, the artist tried to persuade Mrs. Babbitt to purchase canvas. Refusing, she sent him to the woodshed to find some boards, and the result was this captivating likeness.[1]

Similar dramas were often enacted between artists

*Cat.6;
photograph
by Ken
Burris*

occasions, Fuller found himself in the same position as the unfortunate artist in the Babbitt household. During a visit to Brattleboro in 1842, Fuller received few commissions and wrote home that he was painting "miniatures cheap...rather awful events." His father responded with a loan of $15.00 to pay the overdue bill at Mr. Smith's Stage House so that the artist could leave to fill commissions in New Hampshire.[4]

Augustus Fuller's uncle, Nathan Negus (cat. 59), also a portrait painter, recorded in lively detail the mortification of finding himself unable to pay his rent. Writing home to explain why he had failed to make a promised visit, he described this encounter with the Swift family:

> Not having a face to leave until I had paid my bill, my abode now became a voluntary prison. The family, which consisted of three old maids and unmerciful gossips, on finding out my embarassed situation now began to gall my feelings with insulting and disrespectful insinuations. I shall not undertake to describe the wretchedness of my situation.[5]

It is not hard to imagine similar tensions in the Babbitt household in 1836. However acrimonious the situation may have been, its result enriches the genre of non-academic portraiture and our understanding of the forces at work within it.

[1] Recollection of Miss Genevieve Babbitt Hardy (granddaughter of Francis Carlisle Babbitt), December, 1980, research files of Shelburne Museum, Shelburne, Vt.
[2] Augustus Fuller to Aaron Fuller, 24 January 1843, Fuller/Negus Papers, Archives of American Art, 17.49/17.84, microfilm roll # 611, hereafter cited as Fuller/Negus Papers.
[3] Augustus Fuller to Aaron Fuller, 29 January, 1844, Fuller/Negus papers.
[4] Augustus Fuller to Aaron Fuller, 30 July 1842, Fuller/Negus papers.
[5] Nathan Negus to his family, July 1824, Fuller/Negus papers

and their landlords. One of the first necessities for an itinerant artist in a new town was finding lodging; however, his ability to pay rent depended on success in securing commissions. Artists occasionally negotiated to exchange portraits for accommodations. In 1843, Augustus Fuller (cats. 2,4,25,33,34,45,77,78) stayed at Lowell's Farmer and Mechanic House in trade for painting two portraits.[2] In Boston a year later, he moved from Pemberton House to Mr. Pierce's at 13 Gouch Street, because "he owes me fifteen dollars," a sum equivalent to the cost of two portraits.[3] On other

7.
WILLIAM BALCH
Unknown Artist
Mass. or R.I., c. 1820-30
Wove paper, black silk, printer's ink
3 3/4 x 3 1/2 (9.6 x 8.9)
Old Sturbridge Village

SILHOUETTES WERE THE MOST expedient and inexpensive form of portraiture available to New

Englanders in the early 19th century. Profiles were so cheap, costing about ten cents apiece, that an artist's profit was dependent on making them as quickly as possible.[1] The use of a block-printed body in this silhouette would have hastened production while adding a level of detail impossible to achieve by cut paper alone.

While other examples of hollow-cut silhouettes with pre-printed male or female bodies exist, this silhouette is differentiated by the printed name.[2] That personalizing detail may have been added after the body was printed; however, the alignment of the body with the name, and the even density of the ink, suggests that they were printed simultaneously. A printing block with the torso and "WM: BALCH" may have been specially made to produce multiples of this silhouette, perhaps as memorials. Another possibility suggested by the erratic registration of the letters and mismatched type styles is that there was a slot to receive type beneath the woodcut of the torso so that a name could be added.

[1] Rufus Porter's Broadside (fig. 13), c. 1818-1820, lists a price of $.20 for "a common profile cut double". Collection of the American Antiquarian Society, Worcester, Mass.
[2] For other examples of silhouettes with printed bodies see, *American Folk Portraits...from the Abby Aldrich Rockefeller Folk Art Collection*, ed. Beatrix Rumford (Boston: Little, Brown and Company, 1981), 245-246.

Cat. 7

8.
LEWIS FORD BALDWIN (1809-1895)
H. T. Webb
Milford, Conn., 1841
Oil on canvas
28 1/8 X 24 1/4 (71.5 X 61.6)
Inscribed verso: *H. T. Webb/1841 Pinxt Aged 32*
Baldwin Family Collection

EVERY PORTRAIT REPRESENTS a set of choices by the sitter about how he or she wished to be represented. The consciously constructed self-image is evident in this portrait, which presents the incongruous sight of a man posed in his best suit of custom-made clothes while holding a work tool—in this instance a shoemaker's size stick. Chances are that Lewis Baldwin never worked in his shoe shop wearing this formal attire, nor would he carry his tools to church on Sunday. However, it was obviously important to him

Cat.8

to have both aspects of his life recorded in his portrait.[1] The shoemaker's tool expresses his identity as a tradesman, and his erect bearing and stylish clothes bespeak prosperity and his observance of the rules of polite society.

In the 1840s, the mass production of shoes was an important industry in Milford, Conn. An 1845 report on manufactures lists the production of 55,224 pairs of shoes worth $41,706 in the town. The 75 males and 100 females employed in the Milford shoe industry that year[2] were organized in an outwork system in which women bound the leather shoe uppers and male shoemakers stitched the uppers to the soles.

In such a community, the size stick held by Lewis Baldwin would have been readily understood as a symbol of his work as a shoemaker. Size sticks, or foot measures, were flat strips of hardwood, calibrated in shoe sizes, with a fixed stop at one end and a sliding stop at the other.[3] As with modern foot measures, a person's shoe size was determined by resting the heel against the fixed stop and adjusting the other stop to rest against the toe. As a size stick was only needed when a pair of shoes was being custom-made, it is intriguing that he holds a gauge, as mass-produced shoes in standard sizes were exported from Milford.

Cat. 9

Baldwin may have specifically selected the size stick to indicate that he was engaged in custom work, unlike dozens of other Milford shoemakers.

[1] There is a companion to this portrait depicting Mary Fenn, whom Baldwin married in 1841. The newlyweds commissioned their likenesses from H. T. Webb, an artist whose only known works come from coastal Conn. See, George C. Groce and David H. Wallace, *The New York Historical Society's Dictionary of Artists in America 1564-1860* (New Haven and London: Yale University Press, 1957), 667; Jean Lipman and Alice Winchester, *Primitive Painters in America* (New York, 1950), 181.
[2] Federal Writers' Project, *History of Milford, Conn., 1639-1939* (The Milford Tercentenary Committee, 1939), 73.
[3] R. A. Salaman, *Dictionary of Leather-Working Tools, c. 1700-1950* (New York: Macmillan Publishing Company, 1986), 152.

9.
PERLEY BARTLETT (1807-1887)
Unknown artist
Probably Shrewsbury, Mass., c. 1831-35
Oil on canvas
37 x 33 (94 x 83.9)
Sterling Historical Society, Inc., Sterling, Mass.

10.
PERSIS BARTLETT (1808-1899)
Unknown artist
Probably Shrewsbury, Mass., c. 1831-35
Oil on canvas
37 x 33 (94 x 83.9)
Sterling Historical Society, Inc., Sterling, Mass.

IN THE 1960S A DESCENDANT of the Bartlett family found these paintings rolled up in an attic among other family possessions. Unfurling the canvases revealed these rare, unfinished portraits, in which the bodies and background are roughly sketched but the faces of the sitters are almost fully rendered. The female subject is Persis Bartlett, a young woman formally attired in a black dress with her shoulders bared and her hair fashionably styled. The companion portrait is of her husband, Perley Bartlett, on whom a shawl-collared tailcoat and a stock have been outlined. The style of the portraits and the clothes depicted in them suggest that they were begun in the early 1830s. The artist is not known, but they were probably painted in Shrewsbury, Mass., where Perley and Persis were married in 1831.[1]

Why the two portraits were never finished is a

mystery. An incomplete portrait can sometimes be explained by a death in the family, but not in this case, for both Bartletts lived into the late 19th century. Possibly the artist died while working on the paintings, or more likely some exigency forced him to leave town before completing the pair. As there is no evidence that financial or family problems interrupted the portrait sitting, the Bartletts may have felt the likenesses were unsuccessful and terminated the commission.

Today the portraits of Perley and Persis Bartlett are a useful aid to understanding the artistic process of a non-academic portrait painter. The artist began by sketching in the backgrounds and bodies to establish the portrait composition and then focused on the delineation of the faces. The detailed rendering of faces, so essential to a "correct likeness" and so characteristic of non-academic portraiture, has led historians to speculate that itinerant artists pre-painted bodies on canvases and then painted in faces as they received commissions.[2] The Bartlett portraits clearly refute that idea.

The fact that each portrait is in approximately the same incomplete state suggests that the artist worked on them simultaneously. The approach taken in painting a pair of portraits varied according to the artist, the available time, and the needs of the sitters. For example, William Matthew Prior's likenesses of Jesse and Lucy Hartshorn (cats. 42, 43) were both finished on 24 February 1836, but his portraits of William and Nancy Lawson (cats. 53, 54) were completed more than a week apart on the second and eleventh of May 1843. Nathan Negus seems generally to have preferred completing portraits one at a time. On a visit to Fitchburg in 1820 he "inlay'd Esq Willards portrait" on 9 June, took a second sitting with Mr. Willard the following day, and finished the picture on the 12th "much to the satisfaction of all concerned." Two weeks later he began work on Mrs Willard's portrait, which required four days to finish.[3] The term "inlay'd," consistently used by Negus to denote the start of a new painting, seems to describe outlining such as that in the Bartlett portraits. Perley and Persis probably had only one sitting before work on the paintings stopped.

The portraits were very likely commissioned at the time of their marriage, or shortly thereafter. By the early 1830s, Perley Bartlett was a prominent and active

businessman, having bought his own store after working from the age of eighteen for other merchants. In 1837, Perley Bartlett purchased a dry goods business from Manassah Houghton in Sterling, Mass., and moved with his wife and family to that town.[4] Shortly thereafter, the Bartletts commissioned Jones Fawson Morris (cat. 66), a local artist, to paint a group portrait of their three children.[5] It is interesting that the Bartletts chose to have their children's likenesses taken while their own portraits remained incomplete. The style of the children's portrait is so dissimilar from the unfinished paintings that they cannot be attributed to Morris.

[1] Franklin P. Rice, *The Vital Records of the Town of Bolyston, Mass., To the end of the year 1850* (Worcester, Mass: Published by Franklin P. Rice, 1900), 55, 99.
[2] Jean Lipman, *American Primitive Painters* (New York: Oxford University Press, 1942), 19.
[3] Nathan Negus Memorandum Book for 1819, 1820, and 1821, Fuller/Negus Papers.
[4] Obituary of Perley Bartlett, Bartlett Research File, Sterling Historical Society.
[5] Portrait of Bartlett children, c. 1838, collection of the Sterling Historical Society.

Cat.10

11.
SELF-PORTRAIT OF RUTH HENSHAW
BASCOM (1772-1848)
Ashby, Mass., c. 1830
Pastel on paper
18 3/8 x 13 1/4 (46.6 x 33.6)
Old Sturbridge Village

THROUGHOUT THE 19TH CENTURY, most women's lives were focused on marriage, raising children, and managing a household. For housewives, any artistic skills cultivated in their teens, such as ornamental needlework or watercolor painting, were employed in adulthood only as a source of pleasant pastimes.

Cat. 11

However, a few women, like Ruth Henshaw Bascom (cats. 20, 21, 23, 40, 41, 55, 60), Caroline Negus (cats. 73, 74), and Ruth Whittier Shute (fig. 2), actively maintained or developed their artistic talents after marriage. These women became professional artists who supported themselves by taking likenesses.

In Ruth Henshaw Bascom's self-portrait, the artist represented herself as a mature, strong, and confident woman. Her actions throughout her life, recorded in the journals she maintained faithfully from 1789 to 1846, attest to the accuracy of this portrayal.[1] Around the time that she took her own likeness, in late middle age, Bascom had begun working as an itinerant artist. In the winter of 1828, her husband, the Reverend Ezekiel Bascom, made the first of what became annual trips to the South for his health. During the several months of his absence, Bascom worked as a traveling portraitist, visiting friends and relatives around New England. Her decision to work rather than accompany her husband seems to have been motivated by economic considerations, her love of drawing, and her desire to spend time with members of her extended family.

Working for pay was not a new experience for Bascom. Prior to her first marriage in 1804 to Dr. Asa Miles, she worked as a school teacher and a milliner. To prepare to teach, she attended the academy in her hometown of Leicester, Mass., from 1791 to 1793. At the Academy she studied reading, writing, arithmetic and geography; there was apparently no art instruction at the time.[2] Ruth first taught summer session at a district school in 1792 and then for the next eight years. Bonnetmaking and sewing provided a supplement to her income, as they did through her brief marriage to Dr. Miles, her widowhood, and her union with the Reverend Mr. Bascom, whom she married in 1806.

In her journals, Bascom does not mention any artistic endeavors until 19 February 1801, when she "spun some and cut out profiles." The year before she had befriended the artist Ethan Allen Greenwood at the Academy, and he may have prompted her to try making profiles. Through the first decades of the century her journal contains sporadic references to cutting profiles, but it was not until 1819 that taking likenesses became a regular activity for her. That year she noted doing thirty portraits, usually during evening visits with friends. For the next several years references to her art remain mingled with her descriptions of her daily responsibilities as a minister's wife and stepmother to Ezekiel's daughter and an orphaned nephew.

In 1828, when her children had left home and her

husband began to spend winters away from New England, the volume of Bascom's work increased greatly. She took some eighty portraits and, for the first time, was paid. From that point forward, she detailed in her diary purchases of art supplies, the time she spent on profiles, and changes in her method of working. At the end of that year her time was so filled by her artwork that she contemplated giving up her diary.[3] However, she maintained the daily report until 1846, and in it recorded roughly one thousand portraits.

[1] Ruth Henshaw Bascom Diaries, 1789-1846, American Antiquarian Society, Worcester, Mass.
[2] Mary Eileen Fouratt, "Ruth Henshaw Bascom, Itinerant Portraitist," *Itinerancy in New York and New England, Annual Proceedings of the Dublin Seminar for New England Folklife*, ed. Peter Benes (Boston: Boston University Press, 1986), 191.
[3] Ruth Henshaw Bascom Diaries, 31 December 1828.

12.
ALMIRA DODGE BASSETT (1802-1838)
Erastus Salisbury Field (1805-1900)
Lee, Mass., c. 1836
Oil on canvas
35 x 28 1/2 (88.2 x 72.4)
Shelburne Museum, Shelburne, Vt.

13.
JOSEPH BASSETT (1801-1873)
Erastus Salisbury Field (1805-1900)
Lee, Mass., c. 1836
Oil on canvas
34 3/4 x 28 1/2 (88.9 x 72.4)
Shelburne Museum, Shelburne, Vt.

DURING THE SUMMER OF 1836, Erastus Salisbury Field traveled to western Massachusetts, where he obtained portrait commissions in the towns of Lee, Egremont, Stockbridge, Pittsfield, and Great Barrington. A large group of portraits of members of the Bassett family of Lee is credited to this trip because of their similarity to other documented examples of Field's work. Especially distinctive are the artist's use of a soft grey background color, the shaded halo of space that surrounds his subjects' heads, and his attention to fine detail such as the lace that surrounds Almira Bassett's face.[1]

The Bassett portraits demonstrate how artists work-

Top: Cat. 12; below Cat. 13; photographs by Ken Burris

ed through family networks to secure commissions. Among the members of the family recorded by Field were Joseph's parents (cats. 14, 15), his uncle, two cousins by marriage (cat. 29), and his cousin's son.[2]

These paintings preserve the likenesses of one of Lee's founding families. Joseph's parents and Almira's grandparents were among the town's original settlers, who went there from southeastern Massachusetts as the American Revolution was ending.[3] These pioneers established farms and businesses that provided security for themselves and prosperity for their offspring. Forty years after settling in Lee, Joseph's father gave his youngest son and new daughter-in-law a house on the town common.[4]

The Bassetts's portraits probably hung in the parlor of this fashionable Greek Revival house. When the couple sat for these likenesses they had been married for thirteen years and were the parents of two sons and a newborn daughter.[5] Joseph Bassett was an established cabinetmaker, and it is possible that the chair and sofa illustrated in the portraits were products of his shop. Field's formulaic depictions of seated figures have prompted speculation that the furnishings in his portraits were artist's props. While Field often depicted similar wood-finished fancy chairs, they are not identical, showing clear differences in construction, finish, and shape. These chairs reflect the wide range of moderately priced, mass-marketed furniture that filled the parlors of middle-class New Englanders in the 1830s.

These portraits were intended to be lasting images of the Bassetts, but they show how portraitists inevitably captured each subject at a specific point in time. Had Field visited Lee at the end of 1838, he would have painted a widowed Joseph Bassett, Almira having died that year.[6] A decade later he would have found Joseph married to Juliette Hollister Flinn.[7]

A constant in Joseph's adult life was his work as a cabinetmaker. Through the decades, his business prospered and grew, reflecting changes in the furniture industry. When Lee's first cabinetmaker, Abner Taylor, died in 1853, Joseph absorbed his business.[8] Fourteen years later the local newspaper announced that Bassett was establishing a furniture ware-room by moving his shop, a barn, and the "Old Perry Store" to the yard of his residence.[9] There he continued as a cabinetmaker, but also sold mass-produced furniture and provided the services of upholsterer and undertaker.[10] After Joseph's death in 1873, his "desirable old stand," a "large furniture establishment," was purchased by Mr. S.P. Millard, a cabinetmaker who continued to make and repair furniture.[11]

[1] Mary Black, *Erastus Salisbury Field: 1805-1900* (Springfield, Mass: Museum of Fine Arts, 1984), 20.
[2] Portraits of Anselm Bassett and Henry Carlton Hulbert are cited in Black, *Field*, 100; Amos Geer Hulbert appears as fig.14, p.41.
[3] *The Centennial Celebration and Centennial History of the Town of Lee, Mass.*, comp. C.M. Hyde and Alexander Hyde (Springfield, Mass: Clark, Bryan and Co., 1878), 129, 314; a 20th-century label on the back of the portrait of Almira Bassett includes the information: "Granddaughter of John and Martha Crosby, who moved with their family in 1780 to Cape St., Lee, Mass. from Barnstable, Mass."
[4] Architectural Survey Form Number 65, Lee Historical Commission, Public Library, Lee, Mass.; an early 20th-century inscription on the back of the portrait of Nathaniel Bassett (cat. 14) notes that he "built his son Joseph the house where Chas. Hollister (a descendant) now lives."
[5] The Bassett children were Charles Henry (1824), James Watson (1829), and Julia Frances (1836).
[6] *Vital Records of Lee, Mass., to the Year 1850* (Boston: New England Historic Genealogical Society, 1903), 181; works in this series cited hereafter as *V.R.*
[7] A 20th-century label on the reverse of Joseph Bassett's portrait records: "for second wife he married Mrs. Juliette Hollister Flinn September 12, 1848."
[8] *History of Berkshire County, Mass., with Biographical Sketches of Its Prominent Men*, II (New York: J.B. Beers & Co., 1885), 150-151.
[9] *The Valley Gleaner*, 23 May 1867.
[10] Berkshire County, Mass., Probate Records, Court House, Pittsfield, Docket #11823.
[11] *The Valley Gleaner and Berkshire Farmers' Advocate*, 19 March 1874.

14.

NATHANIEL BASSETT

14.

BETHIAH SMITH BASSETT (1761-1849)
Erastus Salisbury Field (1805-1900)
Lee, Mass., c. 1836
Oil on canvas
35 x 28 11/16 (88.9 x 72.9)
Smith College Museum of Art, Northampton, Mass.
Plate 6

15.

NATHANIEL BASSETT (1757/8-1846)
Erastus Salisbury Field (1805-1900)
Lee, Mass., c. 1836
Oil on canvas
35 x 28 5/8 (88.9 x 72.7)
Smith College Museum of Art, Northampton, Mass.
Plate 7

EARLY IN THIS CENTURY a descendant of Nathaniel Bassett outlined her great-grandfather's life history on the back of his portrait. The inscription begins: "Nathaniel Bassett—7th generation from Williams, who came over in ship Fortune, with his wife Elizabeth Tilden 1621."[1] This description of the

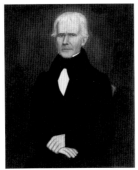

Cat. 14   *Cat. 15*

Bassett lineage shows the same pride in kinship that prompted the commissioning of a large group of family portraits in 1836. That year, on a visit to Lee, Mass., Erastus Salisbury Field took the likenesses of at least eight Bassett relatives (see cats. 12, 13, 29), members of one of the town's most prominent families. To some extent that prominence derived from the Bassetts's part in establishing the town, an event that elevated Nathaniel to the status of family patriarch and became a seminal moment in the shaping of the family's identity.

The town of Lee was incorporated in 1778, and Nathaniel Bassett, his brother Anselm, and his cousin Cornelius settled there shortly afterwards.[2] In 1781, Nathaniel returned to his birthplace of Sandwich, Mass., to marry Bethiah Smith, and moved with his bride to Lee in 1783 after a two-year residence in neighboring Lenox Furnace. Nathaniel had recently completed a period of distinguished military service with the Continental Army. His role in foiling Benedict Arnold's conspiracy with Major André became well known to the citizens of Lee, who hailed him as a local hero. A blacksmith and the town sexton, he was esteemed as a man of industry and commitment to his community.[3] Nathaniel Bassett's portrait epitomizes this life experience, showing a mature man whose face and bearing reveal a character shaped by his 78 years.

Similarly, Bethiah Bassett's portrait depicts a prosperous matriarch, proud of her achievements as wife and mother of ten children, nine of whom lived to adulthood.[4] Her portrait shows an aging woman adorned with an elaborate cap and an imported silk brocade shawl. Field's rendering of these accessories is as detailed as his depiction of her face, clearly shown with a mustache and a pronounced double chin, unmistakable marks of her age.

Both of the Bassetts survived a full decade beyond their portrait sitting. Nathaniel died in 1846 after a fall from the garret stairs.[5] Bethiah lived out the remainder of her life with a generous widow's portion allowing her half of her house, all the household furniture, use of a cow, and financial support from her sons.[6]

[1] Inscriptions on reverse of portraits give biographical information prepared by "N.B.M" (daughter of James Watson Bassett).
[2] *Centennial History of Lee*, 314; *Bassett Genealogy*, unpublished manuscript, private collection.
[3] *Centennial History of Lee*, 152-154, 237, 314, inscription on reverse of portrait of NB.
[4] *V.R.*, Lee, 15-17, 181-183.
[5] *V.R.*, Lee, 181.
[6] Berkshire County, Mass., Probate Records, Courthouse, Pittsfield, Docket #6922.

16.
ESTHER BELCHER BIRD (1792-1840)
Unknown Artist
Foxborough, Mass., c. 1830-1835
Oil on canvas
29 7/8 x 24 (75.9 x 61)
Old Sturbridge Village

THIS PORTRAIT WAS PAINTED when Esther Bird, the wife of Warren Bird and mother of six daughters, was in her early forties.[1] On the back of the portrait is a paper label bearing the inscription: "put on cap when first baby was born in 1814. Old woman then." This articulation of the implicit link between the cap and the wearer's stage of life explains the eye-catching cap in this portrait. It was customary for New England women to begin wearing caps, for social as well as work situations, after marriage or the birth of their first child. The cap signified the transition into adulthood and expressed a woman's role as a wife and mother. The writer Lucy Larcom recalled that her mother had:

> soft, dark, curling hair, which she kept up under her lace-cap-border. Not even the eldest child remembered her without her cap, and when some of us asked her why she never let her pretty curls be visible, she said, "Your father liked to see me in a cap. I put it on soon after we were married, to please him; I always have worn it, and I always shall wear it, for the same reason."[2]

Mrs. Larcom's comments reveal that the donning of

Similarly, Bird's fully covered neck and shoulders would be expected for a woman of her age, for it was thought immodest for any but the young to reveal the back and bosom.[4] Just as the covered shoulders communicate information, so do the accessories. The decoratively embroidered white collar was doubtlessly an example of Mrs. Bird's needlework, and her handsome silk shawl must have been a valuable and prized possession.

Esther Belcher Bird's attire was consciously chosen to express her place in society and her specific life situation. In the 1830s, a person unacquainted with Esther Bird would have seen in her portrait a woman of the middle-class, in early middle age, who was a wife and mother committed to the domestic arts.

[1] Esther Belcher and Warren Bird married in Foxborough, Mass., on 25 November 1813; their six children were: Mary Boyden (1814), Catharine Emma (1817), Clementina Luthera (1819), Esther Belcher (1823), Angeline Cordelia (1826), and Ann Eliza (1828). *V.R.*, Foxborough.
[2] Lucy Larcom, *A New England Girlhood* (Boston & New York: Houghton, Mifflin & Co., 1891), 25-26.
[3] Eliza Leslie, *The House Book; or, a Manual of domestic economy. For town and country, 6th ed.* (Philadelphia: Carey & Hart, 1843), 407.
[4] *The Mirror of the Graces, or The English lady's costume...* (Calcutta: G. M. Anderson, 1817), 57-59.

Cat. 16

caps was governed not by an explicit rule, but by a tacit understanding that the cap was a culturally understood expression of a woman's obligations.

An early-19th-century viewer of this portrait would have read it with a keen eye for such details of dress. Equally expressive are Bird's black dress and the layered shawl and collar covering her shoulders. Each of these garments would have been considered well chosen for Bird's age and situation. In the early 19th century, propriety was the key index to good fashion. Clothing deemed proper suited the wearer's age, figure, complexion, economic means, and social position. Esther Bird's simple but stylish black dress suggests a mature woman with limited means spent wisely on clothing appropriate for a wide range of social situations. As Eliza Leslie advised women:

> For a very lasting dress, nothing is more durable than a thick, double width, India black satin....Ladies who are no longer young always look best in dark-coloured dresses ...and when decidedly old, there is no colour so proper for them as black.[3]

17.
TIRZAH WAITE BOWDOIN (1786-?)
David Waite Bowdoin (c. 1819-c. 1872)
New Braintree, Mass., 1840
Oil on canvas
30 9/16 x 25 7/8 (77.6 x 65.8)
Inscribed on stretcher:
Tirzah Waite, wife of James Bowdoin/taken 1840.
Old Sturbridge Village
Plate 24

18.
JAMES BOWDOIN (1788-1865)
David Waite Bowdoin (c. 1819-c. 1872)
New Braintree, Mass., 1840
Oil on canvas
30 1/8 x 25 7/8 (76.5 x 65.8)
Inscribed on stretcher: *James Bowdoin/taken January 1840 by D. W. Bowdoin.*
Old Sturbridge Village
Plate 25

IN 1901, DURING THE OBSERVANCE of the one hundred and fiftieth anniversary of the incorporation of the town of New Braintree, these portraits were displayed in the town hall as part of "a collection of relics of the first part of the last century."[1] Painted by David Waite Bowdoin, they depict his parents, "prominent and influential" residents of New Braintree.[2] "From the first settlement...it has been strictly an agricultural town," noted a speaker at the sesquicentennial celebration. "We have, all of us, followed the plough, swung the scythe, raked the hay, husked the corn, milked the cows, and known the farmer's life and the farmer's fare."[3]

Certainly James and Tirzah Bowdoin knew both well, yet their portraits do not illustrate their agricultural life, but only the prosperity it yielded. Both subjects greet viewers with confident gazes and good humor, visible in Tirzah's suppressed smile and James's wry grin and twinkling eye. Their clothing—her stylish beige silk dress and ruffled cap trimmed with silk ribbons, his pink silk brocade vest—expresses affluence and panache. Balancing James Bowdoin's dashing presence is the Bible in his hand, which may reflect his Christian beliefs or his role as the family patriarch, represented by the family record maintained in the Bible. Everything about the couple bespeaks prosperity, while the New Braintree context of the portraits implies that it was gained through farming.

The Bowdoin farm was, indeed, productive and prosperous. Comprising roughly 200 acres, it housed, at one time, 19 cows, 2 oxen, 5 horses, and 7 hogs.[4] The large number of cows indicates that the Bowdoins were actively involved in commercial dairying, the prime agricultural activity in New Braintree. This enterprise would have been largely Tirzah's domain, for: "this was at a time when...a man's fortune was in the hands of his wife to that extent that her success or failure to make good cheese was an important factor in his success."[5] The 1847 valuation of their farm at $8588 places it among the most substantial properties in New Braintree. In later years, James Bowdoin was assisted in its management by William, the youngest of his two children. Ultimately, the senior Bowdoin deeded William most of the property, retaining only one quarter of it, which was left to Tirzah and his eldest son, David, when James died in 1865. David had long since left New Braintree to pursue his career as an artist-entrepreneur, and so sold his inherited lands to

his younger brother.[6]

A banner commemorating New Braintree's leadership in dairying, painted by David Bowdoin, was also among the objects displayed in the sesquicentennial exhibition of 1901. The banner had been carried in 1840 by members of the New Braintree Cheese Association during a political rally for William Henry Harrison. Sadly, the banner was destroyed when the Town Hall burned in 1977, but vivid descriptions of it survive. Measuring three and a half by five feet, it was emblazoned with a portrait of Harrison, identified as "Our Candidate and Defender," and framed by the slogan "Our Cause is Our Country." On the reverse side of the banner were two large cheeses, one of which was cut with a knife bearing the word "Whig" on its blade.[7] The banner was preserved by a leading businessman in town because it was an icon of the industry, and of the prosperity brought by New Braintree's leadership in dairying.

Cat. 17

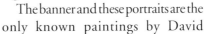

The banner and these portraits are the only known paintings by David Bowdoin. The description of the banner and the flat, detailed rendering of the portraits suggest that he was trained in the tradition of ornamental painting and, like most artisan-painters, applied his craft to everything from signs to likenesses. However, to historians, Bowdoin is better known as a daguerreotypist. Less than a decade after the invention of the daguerrean photographic process, David Bowdoin had adopted that portrait medium. By 1846 he had a studio at 289 Essex Street in Salem, Mass., and within a decade he moved his business to Tremont Street in Boston.[8]

Cat. 18

It was not uncommon for artisan-painters to make the transition to photography as the 19th century, and technology, progressed. For craftsmen like Bowdoin, the daguerreotype provided a portrait medium that was fast, cost-effective, extremely accurate in its representation, and in demand with the public.[9] Painters brought entrepreneurial ability, experience in composing portraits, and an understanding of the importance of a correct likeness to their work as daguerreotypists. Unlike the technicians and businessmen who took up the new craft, portraitists such as Bowdoin were appreciated for the sensitivity and care with which they approached their work.[10]

[1] Charles A. Gleason, "Address of Welcome," *Account of the Observance of the One Hundred and Fiftieth Anniversary of the Incorporation of the Town of New Braintree, Mass.* (Worcester: Charles A. Hamilton, 1902), 11.
[2] Gleason, "Address," 67.
[3] Gleason, "Address," 11.
[4] *Schedule of the Valuation and Taxes in the Town of New Braintree in 1847* (Barre, 1847). Note: As James Bowdoin divided his farm with his son William in 1847, these figures are derived by combining the tax assessments for father and son. Thanks to Holly Izard for sharing her knowledge of farm families in 19th-century Worcester County.
[5] Gleason, "Address," 12.
[6] Worcester County, Mass., Deeds, Courthouse, Worcester, James Bowdoin to William Bowdoin, 423: 352; William Bowdoin to James Bowdoin, 423: 355; David W. Bowdoin to William Bowdoin, 713: 493 (microfilm, Old Sturbridge Village Research Library). Probate Records, Will of James Bowdoin, 4 April 1853, Case #6416.
[7] "Old Fashioned Girls, Lots of them Present at Colonial Hall opening in New Braintree," *Worcester Telegram,* 2 May 1901.
[8] Edward Daland Lovejoy, "Daguerreotypes in America," *Essex Institute Historical Collections,* 81 (April 1945): 190; *The Boston Directory for the Year 1855* (Boston: George Adams, 1855).
[9] For a case study of an artist who made this transition, see: Randolph J. Ploog, "The Account Books of Isaac Augustus Wetherby: Portrait Painter/Photographer," *History of Photography,* 14 (January-March 1990): 77.
[10] Frederic A. Sharf, "'A More Bracing Morning Atmosphere': Artistic Life in Salem, 1850-59," *Essex Inst. Hist. Coll.,* 95 (April 1959): 154.

Cat. 19

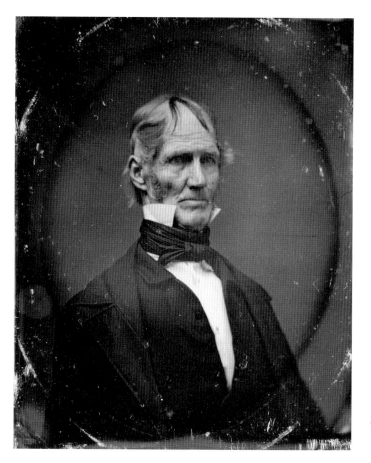

19.
ELIJAH WOODWARD CARPENTER
(1788-1855)
Unknown artist
Bernardston, Mass., c. 1843-1853
Daguerreotype
3 3/16 x 2 11/16 (8.1 x 6.8)
Inscribed verso: *Elijah W. Carpenter*
Old Sturbridge Village

DR. ELIJAH CARPENTER'S stiff white collar and black cravat, so characteristic of 1830s fashions, suggest that this daguerreotype was taken within a decade of the introduction of the first photographic process in 1839. Residents of Carpenter's western Massachusetts community first learned of this remarkable invention in 1840, when the local newspaper announced:

> THE DAGUERREOTYPE...Each particular shade of the face and dress is given with astonishing exactness, and if the likeness be examined with a microscope, it presents each fiber of the skin![1]

News of the portrait medium was quickly followed by advertisements for photographers offering their services to residents of rural communities. Carpenter may have had his picture taken as early as 1843 by L. C. Champney, who advertised that he was in Franklin County offering "daguerreotype miniatures with all the late improvements in coloring." Two months later, Dr. S. Gates was charging $2.00 to $5.00 for photographic likenesses "warranted to be recognisable at first sight" and taken in less than three minutes. By 1847, Greenfield, the Franklin County seat, had a permanent photography studio operated by Benjamin F. Popkins of Connecticut.[2]

Carpenter and a neighbor, Isaac Burrows, had photographic portraits taken in 1853, which they sent to their sons working on the Rochester and Niagara Falls Railroad. An 1856 entry in a friend's scrapbook recalls:

> One night an unknown artist at Rochester got hold of the daguerreotypes, and before morning, painted them as large as life on the head lamp of the locomotive which was to take out the morning train. In the morning the engineer...came out to start his machine and in passing the head of it was startled to see Dr. Carpenter staring at him.[3]

This amusing reminiscence demonstrates an aspect

of daguerreotypes that had broad and immediate appeal for 19th-century consumers: the new medium's portability and relatively low cost provided mementos that could be quickly made and easily sent to friends and family far from home. The anecdote also reveals the overlap between the new and traditional methods of taking likenesses in the middle decades of the 19th century. The feat of the "unknown artist at Rochester" suggests the presence of a painter still working in the non-academic tradition. The artist was skilled at rendering a convincing likeness quickly, was familiar enough with ornamental painting to use a headlamp for a canvas, and had the modesty and humor to permit such a whimsical application of his art.

The artist who participated in this practical joke may have been accustomed to copying likenesses from photographs. As daguerreotypes became more common, artists often used them as visual aids, shortening or eliminating portrait sittings. For example, Isaac Augustus Wetherby noted in June 1850 that he had "painted Mr. Burtin's whole Family on one Peice [sic] from Daguerreotypes 6 in number." Posthumous portraits were often copied from photographs, as when Wetherby painted a portrait "after death from Daguerreotype."[4] This photograph of Elijah Carpenter served this purpose when it was copied for a memorial lithograph that was published with the sermon preached at his funeral in November 1855.[5]

[1] *Gazette and Mercury* (Greenfield, Mass.) March 1840.
[2] *Gazette and Courier* (Greenfield, Mass.) November 1843; *Gazette and Courier*, January 1844; Suzanne Flynt, "The Local Picture: Photography in 19th-Century Franklin County, Mass." (Deerfield, Mass., Pocumtuck Valley Memorial Association, 1989).
[3] Entry from Gov. Cushman's scrap book, 1856, quoted in Lucy Cutler Kellogg, *History of the Town of Bernardston, Franklin County, Mass.. 1736-1900. With Genealogies.* (Greenfield, 1902), 265-266.
[4] Ploog, "Account Books of I. A. Wetherby," 78.
[5] Kellogg, *History of Bernardston*, 139, 329-330.

20.
CHIN-SUNG (sitting)
Ruth Henshaw Bascom (1772-1848)
Leicester, Mass., 1841
Cut paper
6 3/4 x 4 5/8 (17.2 x 11.7)
Label verso: *Aug. 9, 1841 Ruth Henshaw sketched Chin-Sung, at Dr. Flint's, house where he boarded while he was in Leicester.*
Old Sturbridge Village

21.
CHIN-SUNG (standing)
Ruth Henshaw Bascom (1772-1848)
Leicester, Mass., 1841
Cut paper
8 7/16 x 4 1/4 (21.4 x 10.8)
Label verso: *Chin-Sung studying at Leicester Academy about 1841. Copied from J. A. Denny's journal. Chin-Sung, a Chinese teacher came to this country from China last winter (about 1841) with Dr. Parker the missionary. He is very intelligent, and pleasant, dresses in his native costume, talks English considerably well. Is spending 3 or 4 months here at the Academy studying the English language, and boards at, 'Old Doctor Flints'."*
Old Sturbridge Village

AS THE LABELS on the back of these silhouettes indicate, Chin Sung spent several months in the summer of 1841 at the Leicester Academy, where he studied English. The young Chinese teacher came to

Cat. 20

the United States with the Reverend Peter Parker, M.D., a missionary whom Chin Sung had met in China. After almost a year of travel in the United States, Chin Sung and his sponsor returned "to Pekin China his native place."[1]

Cat. 21

Ruth Henshaw Bascom (cat. 11) met the foreign student through her brother-in-law, Dr. Austin Flint, with whom Chin Sung boarded while he was in Leicester. In August 1841, the recently widowed Bascom went to stay with the Flints. She noted in her journal that "the young Chinese has a wife & one daughter 3 years old & he is 22!"[2]

Leicester's residents were also captivated by their Chinese visitor, judging by Bascom's many references to parties at which Chin Sung was a guest. She mentioned drawing him on several occasions, as when

she "sketched 'Chin Sung' the Chinese young man who boards here."[3] This pair of profiles shows the fine detail Bascom could capture in her silhouettes, but the small scale of these differs from most of her portraits, which were usually life-size profile busts. Perhaps her interest in Chin Sung's "native costume" prompted the change to a full-length format.

Chin Sung excited interest everywhere he went in the United States. On a visit to Washington, D.C., in February 1841, his profile was also taken by the renowned silhouettist Auguste Edouart. That silhouette is similar to Bascom's profile of Chin Sung standing. Edouart's portrait bears a Chinese inscription in which Chin Sung offers this explanation of his pose: "Always chatting/ with his friends/ and looking at the moon/ [Chin Sung] recites a poem."[4]

[1] Ruth Henshaw Bascom Diaries, 20 August 1841, American Antiquarian Society.
[2] Ruth Henshaw Bascom Diaries, 20 August 1841.
[3] Ruth Henshaw Bascom Diaries, 9 August 1841.
[4] Andrew Oliver, *Auguste Edouart's Silhouettes of Eminent Americans, 1839-1844* (Charlottesville: University of Virginia Press, 1977), 205.

22.
PRUDENCE CRANDALL (1803-1890)
Francis Alexander (1800-1880)
Boston, Mass., 1834
Oil on canvas
35 1/2 x 27 (90.2 x 68.6)
Uris Undergraduate Library,
Cornell University, Ithaca, NY

IN APRIL 1834, William Lloyd Garrison, the renowned abolitionist and publisher of the newspaper *The Liberator,* invited Prudence Crandall to sit for a portrait commissioned by the New England Anti-Slavery Society.[1] The previous year Crandall had gained notoriety by reorganizing her school in Canterbury, Conn., for the education of African-American girls. Besieged by the racist attacks of her neighbors, her work was supported by anti-slavery activists around New England. The New England Anti-Slavery Society raised sixty-five dollars to have her portrait painted to exhibit at meetings of anti-slavery associations.[2] Crandall consented to their request, and early in April she visited the Boston studio of Francis Alexander where this likeness was painted.

Like Prudence Crandall, Francis Alexander came from northeastern Connecticut, where he was born in Killingly on 3 February 1800. He received his first art instruction from Alexander Robertson in New York City, and in the early 1820s began working as an itinerant artist in Connecticut. For two years he worked out of a studio in Providence, R.I., and in 1827 he moved to Boston. In 1831 he set out on a European journey to study artistic masterpieces, returning to his Boston studio in 1833. When Alexander and Crandall met in 1834, he was an acclaimed portraitist commanding fees of up to one hundred dollars for his paintings, twenty times what he had received for a portrait as an itinerant artist.[3]

In this painting, Alexander employed the academic conventions of a classical pillar and a swag of red drapery, but his subject is depicted with little romantic embellishment. Crandall sits slightly off-center in the composition, illuminated from the side, and gazing serenely at her viewers. Her fashionably cut dress is extremely simple, as is the transparent silk shawl draped around her shoulders and fastened to her bodice with common pins. Her hair is uncharacteristically plain for the 1830s and absent are all of the frills, brooches, and ribbons that commonly adorned women of the time. She sits calmly, wearing an expression of quiet confidence, holding one accessory, a book.

The events that brought Prudence Crandall into the public eye have been well documented in numerous accounts of her life.[4] Born to Pardon and Esther Carpenter Crandall, Prudence was raised with the Quaker belief that all people are equal in God's eyes. She received her early education at a Friends' school and in 1827 she graduated from the Moses Brown School, a Quaker boarding school in Providence, R.I. She taught at the Brown School and at a school in Plainfield, Conn., until a group of citizens from Canterbury in 1831 invited her to open a private school in that town. With the support of the townspeople, Crandall purchased the Luther Paine House on the Canterbury Green, in which she opened a school for young ladies in January 1832. The curriculum included instruction in reading, writing, arithmetic, English grammar, geography, history, natural and moral philosophy, chemistry, and astronomy.

In the fall of 1832, the school's harmonious and supportive atmosphere evaporated when Sarah Harris, a young African-American girl from the community, was admitted as a student, and the incensed parents of the white students withdrew their daughters. With the support of Garrison and other abolitionists, Crandall reopened her school as an academy for "Young Ladies and Little Misses of Color"[5] on 1 April 1833, admitting students from around New England and the Northeast. As she explained much

Cat. 22

later, "having been taught from early childhood the sin of Slavery, my sympathies were greatly aroused…I made up my mind that if it were possible I would teach colored girls exclusively. I made the attempt, and the result is before the public."[6]

Having failed to persuade Crandall to close the school, enraged citizens from the community petitioned the General Assembly in Hartford to outlaw her actions. On 24 May 1833, a "Black Law" was passed outlawing the establishment of schools "for instruction of colored persons belonging to other states and countries."[7] Crandall was arrested on 27 June 1833 and was jailed for one night in Brooklyn, Conn. Five months later she was convicted for breaking the "Black Law," but the following July the conviction was overruled, as the school pre-dated the law.

At the same time that legal pressure was being exerted, a more direct form of harassment was taking place. Almost from the inception of the school, Canterbury's merchants refused to supply it. The students were taunted when they appeared in public, stones and eggs were thrown at the school, the water supply was fouled with animal feces, and the building was set on fire. The violence mounted steadily until, after Crandall's conviction was overturned, an angry mob attacked the school, shattering most of its windows. Fearing for the safety of her students, Crandall closed the school on 10 September 1834.

Just prior to the climax of these events, Crandall married the Reverend Calvin Philleo. In the aftermath of the mob's attack, the couple acted quickly to disassociate themselves from Canterbury. In November they sold the school house for $2,000 and the following May Prudence and Calvin Philleo left town. Prudence moved steadily westward, residing for a time in New York state and later spending nearly thirty years farming and teaching in Illinois. Following her husband's death in 1874, she moved with her brother to Kansas. In 1886, the Connecticut Legislature, responding to a petition signed by state residents, awarded Prudence Crandall Philleo an annual pension of four hundred dollars. Mark Twain was among those who agitated on her behalf. He also tried to buy the Canterbury house back for her, but she declined his offer, saying she preferred to remain in Kansas, where she died in 1890.

Every first-hand account of Crandall's actions relates that she was motivated by her belief in the equality of all people and a desire to use her gifts to open greater opportunities to African-Americans. She stated that she was never driven by abolitionist zeal, but simply responded to situations in the only ways she felt were morally right. She was noted for her modesty and her refusal to capitalize on the brief fame brought by the episode of 1833-34. It seems fitting that she did not choose to celebrate herself in a painted likeness, as so many New Englanders did; rather, it was respectful

admirers who commissioned this portrait to record permanently the way Prudence Crandall presented herself as the proprietress of her school.

This painting ultimately came into the possession of Crandall's friend and supporter, the Reverend Samuel Joseph May, a prominent abolitionist. Shortly before his death in 1871, May donated his important collection of anti-slavery pamphlets and books to Cornell University. Upon learning of the University's plans to establish a college for women, May also decided to give the school the portrait of Prudence Crandall to serve as an inspiration to its new female students.[8]

[1] Susan Strane, *A Whole-Souled Woman, Prudence Crandall and the Education of Black Women* (New York: W.W. Norton, 1990),138.
[2] Mavis Olive Welch, *Prudence Crandall, A Biography* (Manchester, Conn.: Jason Publishers, 1983), 96; David O. White, "The Life of Prudence Crandall, Chronology of Events," in Randy Ross-Ganguly, *The Prudence Crandall Museum: A Teachers' Resource Guide* (Hartford: The Conn. Historical Commission, 1988), 54.
[3] Groce and Wallace, *Dictionary of Artists in America*, 4.
[4] See biographies by Strane and Welch cited above, as well as accounts in Samuel J. May, *Some Recollections of our Anti-Slavery Conflict* (Boston: Fields, Osgood, 1869), 39-72, and Ellen D. Larned, *History of Windham County, Conn.*, II (Worcester, Mass.: C. Hamilton, 1880), 490-502.
[5] *Vermont Chronicle*, 15 March 1833.
[6] Private letter, 15 May 1869, quoted in Larned, *History of Windham County*, 491.
[7] "The Black Law" published in Ross-Ganguly, *Teachers' Resource Guide*, 65.
[8] Information on the Cornell University Special Collection on Slavery provided by Yoram Szekely, Director of the Uris Undergraduate Library, Cornell, Ithaca, N.Y.

23.
EDWIN DAVIS (1821-?)
Ruth Henshaw Bascom (1772-1848)
North Marlboro, N.H., 1838
Pastel on paper
19 x 13 1/2 (48.2 x 34.3)
Inscribed verso: *Mr. Edwin Davis, N. Marlboro, New Hampshire. Sketched and framed in 1838*
Old Sturbridge Village

RUTH HENSHAW BASCOM (cat. 11) was cutting profiles as early as 1801, but not until 1828, at the age of 56, did she become a professional artist. A year later she began to work as an itinerant, traveling throughout Massachusetts, New Hampshire, and Maine taking likenesses.[1] During a trip to New Hampshire in

Cat. 23

After his ordination, Davis preached in various New England states, including Massachusetts, Vermont, and New Hampshire. Although Davis moved frequently during his career, he served for several years in many of the churches before taking another pastorate. In addition to his active ministry, Davis maintained his commitment to education, often teaching and assisting with the supervision of public schools.[3]

[1] Fouratt, "Ruth Henshaw Bascom," 190-91.
[2] Charles A. Bemis, *History of the Town of Marlborough, Cheshire County, N.H.* (Boston, 1881), 139.
[3] Bemis, *History of Marlborough*, 228-230.

1838, Bascom drew this pastel of Edwin Davis. Then seventeen, Davis was living at home and teaching at the newly established Sunday school of the Baptist Church.[2] This pastel captures a young man facing adulthood: Davis would soon begin to spend his winters as a school teacher in other towns.

Religion and education remained constants in Davis's life. Born in 1821 to Jonah and Sarah Davis of Marlborough, N.H., he was educated in the local district school and began attending Melville Academy in Jaffrey at age fourteen. He started teaching in 1838, and worked in several schools in New England before taking a school in Guilford, Vermont, in 1840. There he met the Reverend W. N. Barber, who encouraged Davis to pursue ordination. He studied under Barber until 1842, when he went to Westmoreland, N.H., to study with the Reverend C. Woodhouse. Davis preached his first sermon in Vernon, Vt., and was ordained at the annual session of the New Hampshire Convention of Universalists at Winchester in 1845. In that year he married Nancy Chase whose acquaintance he had made as a young teacher in Guilford.

24.
ELIZABETH STONE DENNY (1811-1899)
Augustus Fuller (1812-1873)
Worcester, Mass., 1840
Oil on canvas
29 7/8 X 23 7/8
Inscribed verso: *January 20, 1840,/ Augustus Fuller, / Deaf and Dumb Mate*
Worcester Historical Museum, Worcester, Mass.
Plate 8

25.
EDWARDS WHIPPLE DENNY
(1810-1865)
Augustus Fuller (1812-1873)
Worcester, Mass., 1840
Oil on canvas
30 1/4 X 24
Inscribed verso: *January 20, 1840/ Augustus Fuller,/ Deaf and Dumb Mate*
Worcester Historical Museum, Worcester, Mass.
Plate 9

THE ITINERANT PORTRAITIST Augustus Fuller (cats. 33, 34, 45, 77, 78), who was deaf, derived some of his greatest pleasure from visiting with and painting former classmates from the American Asylum for the Deaf and Dumb, which he had attended from 1824 to 1829. The shared experience that bound Fuller to his "deaf and dumb mates" and their mutual knowledge of sign language made these visits easier for him than his exchanges with the hearing population.[1] During a visit to Worcester early in 1840, Fuller painted these portraits of Edwards and Elizabeth Denny, both of whom had attended the Asylum in Hartford from 1825 to 1831.[2]

Fuller showed his friends holding writing implements, evidence of their inability to speak. Not merely signs of deafness, however, these were potent emblems of the Dennys's acquisition of language. In the early 19th century, most people who were deaf were also illiterate, which forced them to live in isolation from all but those who could interpret their gestures. Edwards Denny and his future wife, Elizabeth Stone, were

Cat. 24

among the fortunate few who had the world opened to them by receiving specialized education and learning to read and write. Both Edwards and Elizabeth were enabled by financial support from the state of Massachusetts to study at the American Asylum, a progressive educational institution, which at the time of its founding in 1817 was the only school for the deaf in the United States.[3] From the start, the chief aim of the school was, as the second annual report explained, "the improvement of the pupils in *written language*," because "*this* is the only avenue to the various departments of knowledge which books contain and...is necessary even for the purposes of their common intercourse with mankind."[4] An important part of this instruction was teaching students to communicate through sign language, using the manual alphabet developed in France by Abbé Sicard.

Cat. 25

The expanded curriculum of the early 1820s featured instruction in "mechanical employments among the pupils," with the goal of "qualifying them to obtain a livelihood." In 1825, when Edwards Denny matriculated to the school, there were thirty-seven male students studying different trades, including joinery, cabinetmaking, coopering, cutlery, shoemaking, and tailoring. Probably among the "thirteen engaged in joiner's and cabinet-maker's work," Denny found employment as a woodworker when he left the Asylum.[5] Similarly, Augustus Fuller and three classmates learned to draw and paint at the Asylum, studying with an instructress brought in specially to teach them.[6] Female students also engaged in manual employ-

ments, such as binding shoe uppers and sewing.[7]

The annual reports of the Asylum published essays written by students demonstrating their mastery of language. One essay, "On The Duty of Affording Instruction to the Deaf and Dumb," noted:

Many of the Deaf and Dumb do not attend to school, and are very illiterate, and are also far from being useful members of Society...As the ground is not taken care of, and is uncultivated, so the minds of our brethren are blank and neglected. As the garden is beautiful and filled with beautiful flowers by the industry of a gardener, so shall their minds be also improved; this is possible.[8]

Edwards and Elizabeth Denny's adult lives exemplified the independence and productivity made possible by the Asylum's nurture. Unlike so many of their "brethren" who found marginal employment and lived as dependents in others' households, this couple enjoyed a successful artisan's career and a home of their own.

Denny and Stone disappear from the public record between leaving the Asylum in 1831 and their marriage in 1837. She probably resided with her family in Dorchester, while he established himself as a sash-and-blind maker in Worcester or the neighboring town of Leicester, his family's home. The published announcement of their marriage in Worcester on 4 May 1837 noted that they were "both deaf and mutes, and formerly inmates of the Hartford Asylum for the Deaf and Dumb."[9] Within six months of their marriage, Edwards purchased a building lot, presumably for a house. Six years later he invested in another plot of land just outside the center of Worcester with the specific intent of building a dwelling house.[10]

Between 1837 and 1855, Denny was a sash-and-blind maker, but after 1856, city directories list him as either a woodworker or a carpenter.[11] Yarn swifts labelled "Silk & Cotton/ Reels/ Manufactured By/ Edw. W. Denny,/ Deaf & Dumb/ Worcester, Mass." (fig. 18) show that Denny ultimately had his own business. His shop was "at Merrifield's," and later Court Mill, both large industrial buildings where manufacturers rented space with power.[12]

The Dennys' 1840 portraits show that the couple was prospering even at that early point in their marriage. The pair is seated in fashionable furniture, she in a chair with stylish underscrolled arms and a decorative painted finish, and he on a Grecian sofa covered with figured scarlet plush, an upholstery treatment that was modish and fairly expensive in 1840. Although their clothing does not reflect the most current fashions, both are elegantly attired, and Edwards's garments are tailormade. Within a year of the painting of these affirmative images, the Denny household grew with the birth of a daughter, Ann Elizabeth. She was able to hear, as was her younger brother, Daniel Edward, born in 1845.[13]

Augustus Fuller's pleasure in visiting his school-mates' home may have been tempered by envy, for his correspondence shows that he yearned for the kind of personal happiness the Dennys had found. Although his letters are "full of glory" in his artistic ability and the adventure of his travels, they also convey real loneliness and a longing for companionship and stability.[14] Couples like the Dennys and Aaron and Sophia Fuller, his brother and sister-in-law who also met at the Asylum, offered Augustus evidence that deafness need not be a barrier to a loving partnership and a reminder of his failure to form such a bond.

Fuller's letters also demonstrate, in their style and content, that he never completely mastered written language. His difficulty in communicating was problematic, for success as an itinerant artist depended greatly on entrepreneurship, requiring the ability to pitch one's skills and to bargain. More than once Fuller wrote to his family that "one rascal has told me lies" and that he was cheated out of a full payment on the argument that he had not understood the nego-tiations.[15] Perhaps because of this, a member of Fuller's family would occasionally travel with him. For example, in 1841, his stepbrother, George, accompanied Augustus on a journey to New York state. With George as his agent, the artist enjoyed one of the most productive and profitable periods of his career. He estimated his income as $1000 between January and May, although George's accounts for the same period record a figure closer to $650.[16] On many other occasions, when Aaron Fuller's business took him to Boston or New York state, Augustus would travel with his father. Although the senior Fuller did not transact his son's business, he played a supervisory role on these trips.[17]

Fuller's life as an itinerant artist caused his family in Deerfield, Mass., many worries. Observations in fam-ily letters that Augustus seemed "steady" and his own pledges of "cold water temperance" allude to his battle with alcoholism.[18] In 1851 he was jailed in Spring-field, Mass., for drunken and disorderly behavior. He offered his brother a moving description of the trial, in which he was frustrated by his inability to communi-cate his innocence to the court "by making fingers." He concluded this account with the woeful plea, "God pity this poor ignorant and deaf mute for the world is sin suffering and death."[19] Following this episode his family became increasingly insistent that Augustus return home, and after a few final painting trips he submitted. In resignation, he thenceforth identified himself as "Cranberry Cultivator," no longer "Augustus Fuller — Por-trait Painter."[20]

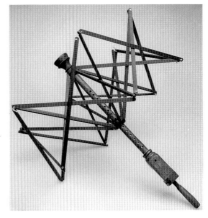

Fuller's portraits of Edwards and Elizabeth Denny represent not two, but three people struggling to overcome the limitations

Above: Fig.18: Yarn swift, Edwards Denny, Worcester, Mass., c.1850, wood, Old Sturbridge Village. At left: detail showing label.

of deafness to lead full and independent lives. At the moment when the portraits were painted, all three were making their way in the hearing world and enjoying good fortune. The difficulties that Augustus Fuller later encountered offer a complement to the Dennys' extraordinary success. He, like most 19th-century New Englanders with hearing impairments, depended on family throughout his life, although he experienced unusual freedom in his travels and earned substantial sums as an artist.

[1] Correspondence of Augustus Fuller, Fuller/Negus Papers; also, Fuller-Higginson Papers, Pocumtuck Valley Memorial Association Library, Deerfield, Mass., hereafter cited as Fuller-Higginson Papers.
[2] *Tenth Report of the Directors of the American Asylum at Hartford for the Deaf and Dumb…May 13, 1826* (Hartford: W. Hudson and L. Skinner, 1826); in the fifteenth *Report* (1831) they are listed among the students who had left the school.

[3] Augustus Fuller also received state support by petitioning the Mass. Legislature, see cat. 45.

[4] *Second Report* (1818), 5.

[5] *Tenth Report*, 4-5.

[6] H. P. Peck to Aaron Fuller, 26 September 1827, Fuller-Higginson Papers, box 1, folder 4.

[7] *Tenth Report*, 5.

[7] *Eleventh Report* (1827), 13.

[8] *Barre Gazette*, 12 May 1837.

[9] Worcester County, Mass., Registry of Deeds, Marshall S. Ballard to Edwards W. Denny, 7 November 1837, 329: 271; Levi Lincoln to Edwards W. Denny, 6 November 1843, 383: 79; Oliver Hall to Edwards W. Denny, 6 November 1843, 383: 80.

[10] Henry J. Howland, *Worcester Almanac, Directory and Business Advertiser* (Worcester: Henry J. Howland, 1845-1865).

[11] *Worcester Almanac...for 1855*, 80; *Worcester Almanac...for 1856*, 103; Charles G. Washburn, *Industrial Worcester* (Worcester: The Davis Press, 1917), 292-293.

[12] *Genealogy of the Denny Family in England and America, Descendents of John Denny of Combs, Suffolk, England, in 1439*, comp. C.C. Denny (Leicester, Mass., 1886), 736-737.

[13] Fanny Fuller to Aaron Fuller, 15 June c. 1832-33, Fuller/Negus Papers.

[14] Augustus Fuller to George Fuller, April 1843, Fuller/Negus Papers.

[15] Augustus Fuller to Fuller family, May 1841, Fuller-Higginson Papers, Box 1, Folder 8; Account by George Fuller of Augustus Fuller's work from December 1840 through May 1841, Box 14, Folder 3.

[16] Aaron Fuller to Fanny Fuller, 3 September 1832, 16 February 1836, Fuller-Higginson Papers, Box 2 Folder 5.

[17] George Fuller to Aaron Fuller, 10 September 1844, Fuller-Higginson Papers, Box 1, Folder 8; Augustus Fuller to Aaron Fuller, 17 June 1842, Fuller/Negus Papers.

[18] Augustus Fuller to George Fuller, 5 April 1851, Fuller/Negus Papers.

[19] Augustus Fuller to George Fuller, 8 November 1855, Fuller/Negus Papers; Augustus Fuller to Aaron Fuller, 11 April 1832, Fuller-Higginson Papers, Box 5, Folder 6.

26.

TIMOTHY DOTY (1788-1835)
SUSAN COWEE DOTY (1809-1879)
PEARSON C. DOTY (1833-?)

Robert Peckham (1785-1877)

Westminster, Mass., c. 1834-35

Oil on canvas

36 1/8 x 50 1/8 (91.7 x 127.3)

Forbush Memorial Library Trustees, Westminster, Mass.

Plate 1

GROUP OR FAMILY portraits are relatively rare in the non-academic oeuvre. More commonly, individual likenesses of a husband and wife were composed to read as a pair, often with the partners facing each other, seated in matching chairs or on either end of a sofa (see cats. 49, 50). That compositional device is used here on a single canvas (which is exactly double the average size of an individual portrait) in order to place the toddler, Pearson, on the sofa between his parents. Timothy Doty, a prosperous and influential businessman in Westminster, Mass., spent most of his adult life alone. At age forty-five he married Susan Cowee, a local woman twenty-one years his junior, who bore him a son on 15 October 1833, ten months after the marriage. The painted record of this new family celebrates Doty's sense of fulfillment, brought by his wife and heir (depicted slightly larger than life for emphasis), along with the more tangible trappings of his success.

The satisfaction so evident in this painting heightens the tragedy of Timothy Doty's death on 9 March 1835, just months after the family's portrait sitting. The fact that he left no will suggests that he died suddenly and unexpectedly. Having died intestate, a detailed inventory was taken of his possessions, recording real estate valued at $4357.00 and personal estate of $6342.96.[1] His substantial holdings included his house and farm, other lots of wood and pasture land, and the contents of the store he had owned and operated for ten years.

Doty began his rise to prominence in 1813, when he purchased the Whitman tavern which he operated with his father until 1824. During his years as an innkeeper he commenced a role as a public servant. This included service as town postmaster, selectman, tax assessor, town moderator, and as a representative in the general court.[2] Doty gave up innkeeping to become a merchant, and the 1835 inventory lists the large and varied stock of his store. The goods included hundreds of yards of fabric, sewing notions, ready-made apparel such as stockings and gloves, tools, table and cook wares, foodstuffs, and a diverse apothecary's pharmacopoeia. His large supply of palm leaves, straw braid, palm leaf hats, and straw bonnets indicate that Doty was also a broker in the hat-making industry that flourished in central Massachusetts in the second quarter of the 19th century.

Doty's business was lucrative and unencumbered by debt. When he died it was transferred intact to his young son. The designation "The Widow Doty's Store," by which the homestead is still known, suggests that Susan Doty took over the operation of her husband's business.[3] However, when she married Milton Joslin in 1841 the couple began to divest themselves of Timothy Doty's property.[4]

When viewed within the context of Doty's wealth and social influence, this painting is a very traditional symbol of status. Like so many other members of the rising middle-class, Doty emulated the ways of the elite in commissioning a portrait to memorialize his achievements. The image abounds with emblems of accomplishment, ranging from the young heir to the elegant household furnishings. Doty's inventory offers persuasive evidence that this portrait depicts their formal parlor with its upholstered sofa, valued at $25, and its elaborate draperies worth $40. Not visible in this picture are the carpet and protective hearth rug, a Grecian center table, Susan Doty's work table, a set of six side chairs, and a looking glass. These were all stylish furnishings, which, like the portrait, were objects that had only recently moved into the economic realm of the middle class.

Similarly, the gold watch, presented in the portrait as a playful distraction for young Pearson, would have been understood by 19th-century viewers as a sign of wealth. Although no longer taxed as in the 18th century, pocket watches were usually owned only by the rich. Indeed, this watch, appraised at $40 in the inventory, was the single most valuable object in Doty's home, but not the only timekeeper. Doty also owned a time piece (valued at $25) and a brass clock (worth $23).

Strong stylistic evidence links this portrait to the hand of Robert Peckham, an artist who, like the Dotys, lived and worked in Westminster. The colors in the Doty family portrait are much brighter and more varied than Peckham's usual palette (see cats. 46, 47) but the crisp delineation and the distinctive modeling of the subjects' foreheads and temples are characteristic of Peckham's work.[5]

Little is known about the start of Peckham's artistic career. One of his earliest works is an accomplished portrait painted c. 1817, showing sixteen members of the artist's family.[6] This group portrait is far more complex in its composition and rendering of space than the painting of the Dotys. While Peckham's work shows artistic sophistication, it also bears the hallmarks of the decorative painter, notably his use of outlining and detailed patterns. Like most non-academic artists, Peckham offered many painting services. In the 1820s he advertised that his Westminster-based business could provide "house, sign, chaise,

chair & ornamental painting, gilding &c.," painted floor cloths, fancy chairs, and portraits painted at patrons's "residences in different towns, or at the shop of the subscribers."[7]

Cat. 26

In 1828 Peckham was appointed deacon of the Westminster First Congregational Church and the following year he sold his painting business.[8] From that point forward, the time he devoted to painting was focused on portraiture. Peckham painted many of Worcester County's citizens, including Susan Doty's cousins, Mr. and Mrs. William Cowee, and her second husband Milton Joslin.[9]

Peckham gradually became involved in the causes of temperance and abolition, and in 1842 he was forced to resign his deaconship due to a controversy over his advocacy of the anti-slavery movement. After that his energies were increasingly directed to social reform.[10] But the years between 1828 and 1842 were among Peckham's most prolific as an artist, and the Doty portrait offers a vivid example of his work during that period.

[1] Worcester County, Probate Records, Inventory of the Estate of Timothy Doty, 28 March 1835, Case #17298, 76: 307-313, .

[2] William Sweetzer Heywood, *History of Westminster, Mass.* (Lowell, Mass.: Vox Populi Press, 1893), 323, 326, 445, 499, 501-502, 504.

[3] *Homestead Heritage of Westminster* (Westminster, Mass.: The Westminster Historical Society, 1980), 100.

[4] Worcester County, Deeds, Pearson C. Doty to various Grantees, 362: 452; 390: 156; 391: 466-8; 392: 246: 394: 193.

[5] Dale T. Johnson, "Deacon Robert Peckham: `Delineator of the Human Face Divine'," *The American Art Journal* (January 1979): 27-36; David Krashes, "Robert Peckham, Portrait Painter of Massachusetts," *Maine Antiques Digest* (January 1985).

[6] Portrait of the Peckham-Sawyer Family, Museum of Fine Arts, Boston; see Laura C. Luckey, "New Discoveries in American Art: An Early Family Portrait by Robert Peckham," *The American Art Journal* (Autumn 1980): 85-86.

[7] *Massachusetts Spy*, 9 May 1827.

[8] Krashes, "Robert Peckham."

[9] Portraits of: Mr. and Mrs. Wm. Cowee, New York State Historical Association, Cooperstown, N.Y.; Milton Joslin, Forbush Memorial Library, Westminster, Mass. The Fruitlands Museum, Harvard, Mass., has a portrait attributed to Peckham of a woman identified as Susan Cowee Doty Joslin; however, this identification is questionable as the painting appears to date to the mid-1830s and shows a middle-aged woman.

[10] Johnson, "Deacon Robert Peckham," 27.

27.

ELIJAH DUDLEY (1803-?)
Zedekiah Belknap (1781-1858)
Shrewsbury, Mass., 1829 & 1838
Oil on canvas
27 5/16 x 23 (69.4 x 58.4)
Inscribed on lower stretcher: *Z. Belknap 1829/Shrewsbury* and: *Finished over in 1838*
Inscribed on upper stretcher (not in artist's hand):
Portrait of Mr. Elijah Dudley
Old Sturbridge Village

THE GHOSTLY SHADOW of an over-painted collar on Elijah Dudley's cheek is a reminder that, in the past, a portrait was often an individual's only fixed image, so tremendous emphasis was placed on its accuracy. A "correct likeness" or a detailed and faithful representation was demanded of non-academic portraitists. Accuracy was important enough to Elijah Dudley that, nine years after his original sitting, he had his portrait "finished over." It was not unusual to modify portraits. When Chester Harding reopened *Cat. 27* his Boston studio after a two-year hiatus, he found that

"many whom I had painted previously wanted their pictures altered, either because the dress was out of fashion, or the expression did not please them."[1] The changes made to Elijah Dudley's portrait updated his appearance to the late 1830s. When he first sat for Zedekiah Belknap (cats. 44, 51, 52) in 1829, he wore what was then a stylish tailcoat with notched lapels, a white cravat, and a shirt with a starched collar projecting well above his jawline. In 1838 the portrait was repainted to show Dudley wearing a modish shawl-collar coat, a black cravat, and the lower, curved shirt collar just coming into fashion. Additionally, his shoulders were broadened slightly and his hairstyle was modified by masking a high curl in the front and adding forward-sweeping tendrils at his temple.

Dudley, a shoemaker, was typical of the middle-class tradesmen who comprised Belknap's clientele. Both men were sons of rural artisans and were born in the same section of southern Worcester County, although Belknap spent most of his childhood in Vermont.[2] The artist traveled primarily in those regions of New England with which he was most familiar—Vermont, central Massachusetts, and southern New Hampshire. An 1807 graduate of Dartmouth College, Belknap studied divinity, but "his only employment...was that of portrait painting."[3] His earliest known work is dated 1810 and the latest was painted in 1848.[4]

Belknap's technique evolved into a formula and many of its elements are evident in the portrait of Elijah Dudley. Scored wooden panels were the artist's preferred painting surface (see cat. 44), but when he used canvas it had the obvious diagonal twill weave visible in this portrait. Belknap used outlining rather than modeling to define form, as seen in his rendering of Dudley's nose, which is thrown into profile by a shadow. Finally, like many of the artist's subjects, Elijah Dudley's seated form is set against a green background with a fall of red drapery behind his left shoulder.

[1] Chester Harding, *My Egotistography* (Cambridge, Mass., 1866), 136-137.
[2] Elijah Dudley, son of Lydia Marble and Jonathan Dudley, (a cooper), born Sutton, Mass., 30 July 1803; Zedekiah Belknap, Jr., son of Elizabeth Wait and Zedekiah Belknap (a tailor), born Auburn, Mass., 8 March 1781.
[3] The Reverend George T. Chapman, *Sketches of the Alumni of Dartmouth College* (Cambridge, Mass., 1867), 131.
[4] Elizabeth R. Mankin, "Zedekiah Belknap," *Antiques,* 110 (November 1976): 1056-1070.

28.
STEPHEN FITCH (1767-1849)
Unknown Artist
Connecticut or New York, c. 1820
Oil on canvas
33 3/16 x 27 7/8 (84.3 x 70.8)
Old Sturbridge Village

STEPHEN FITCH HAD his portrait painted alone, unaccompanied by an image of the woman he had married in his youth. He wears his hat and holds a snuffbox; both were practices increasingly unacceptable in genteel parlors or in the presence of women. His features, too, contrast with the strongly defined faces in most portraits of male New Englanders; there is something both petulant and enigmatic in his rounded features. His depiction cuts against the conventions of respectable representation, just as his life exemplifies darker themes usually absent from portraits and their symbolized stories of achievement, marital and parental commitment, prosperity, and abundance.

Born into one of New Canaan, Conn.'s wealthiest families, Fitch married at seventeen—remarkably young for a man—fathered six children, and operated a prosperous farm comprising two dwelling houses, two barns, and 130 acres.[1] But his family relationships were deeply disturbed from the outset. For twenty-two years he created a domestic hell for his wife Charlotte, beating her, threatening her life with guns, knives, and ropes, and constantly talking of his plans for a murder-suicide. When Charlotte managed to break away, she fled to her family and petitioned for one of Connecticut's rare legislative divorces and for custody of her children. The men of the legislature granted the divorce on the clear evidence that Fitch was a man of "very licentious sentiments and principals," who entertained "an inveterate hatred towards [his wife] and has long since chose her as the object of his cutthroat resentment."[2] But captive to their society's deeply patriarchal assumptions about the family, the Assembly proved unwilling to give Charlotte custody of the children.

In 1808, Stephen Fitch found himself with the care of three sons, aged six to twelve, and his elderly mother, Abigail Reed Fitch. His reputation in New Canaan was ruined and he was burdened with his financial obligation to Charlotte. A lien was placed on

his property to secure the annual alimony payments of $150, an encumbrance which made it hard to sell his real estate.[3] Seeking a way to deal with his disrupted household, Fitch became involved in complex and ultimately unsuccessful arrangements with the Shaker community in New Lebanon, N.Y. He first visited the community on 13 September 1809, returning in the following months professing to have experienced a religious conversion.[4]

By February 1810, the Shakers had agreed to establish a community on Fitch's land. He deeded his

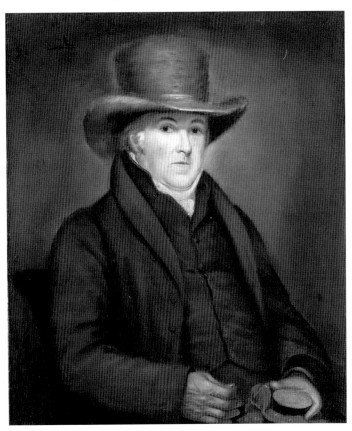

Cat. 28

property to the Shakers for $7,000 and they assumed his alimony payments and the care of his mother and sons.[5] Fitch accepted a note in lieu of cash payment, agreeing that when he called it in the Shakers would have a year or two to pay him. Early in March 1810 a group of eleven Shaker brethren and sisters went to the New Canaan farm "to improve the place" while Fitch moved his family to New Lebanon.[6] The Shakers quickly discovered Fitch's ungovernable personality. Within the community he disobeyed Shaker doctrine by moving his residence "at his own solicitation," and he left the community for periods to transact business.[7] Many at New Lebanon began to suspect that Fitch's conversion was a pretense "done for a trap."[8] On 22 January 1811, less than a year after the original agreement, Fitch demanded immediate payment on his note. Shortly after that, the brethren having concluded that "he is a divel," Fitch was escorted to Albany "to stay there if he will."[9]

The Shakers acted quickly to end their dealings with the Fitch family. When, during a visit to his sons in 1811, Fitch refused to indenture the boys to the Shakers, the members of the community "did not chuse to keep them" and sent the two youngest away with their father.[10] The eldest son, Francis Bushnell, was only permitted to stay because he hid "for fear of his father."[11] A year later the Shakers sold the Fitch farm for $9,000 to Jacob Selleck, a relative of Charlotte Fitch's.[12]

While still ostensibly a resident of the New Lebanon community, Fitch established himself as a merchant and trader in upstate New York. His shrewdness and skill at bargaining suited him to commerce and he quickly made a reputation as an Indian agent. When Fitch and his sons, William and Benjamin, left New Lebanon, they went to Buffalo, where Fitch represented the government in negotiations with Red Jacket, a Seneca chief. The Fitches were still in Buffalo when it was burned by the British in 1813, an event that Benjamin recalled vividly later in life.[13]

Not much is known about Fitch's life from the time his children left his care until his death in Brooklyn in 1849, although he continued his work as a trader. His letters to his sons, written from northern New York state, advise that honesty gains respect.

> Keep yourself out of harm's way, be honest, and at all times speak the truth, be faithful and trustworthy, letting your yea, be yea, and your nay be nay. Don't be guilty, my dear son, of any mean or ungentlemanlike thing or action. But in all things, and in all places, and in whatsoever situation your lot be cast, be the man of honor, yea, the honest gentleman.[14]

These sentiments seem hypocritical coming from a man like Stephen Fitch, but they show that he knew the rules of society and their worth. Fitch also understood that portraits were among the emblems of identity that communicated social status in the early 19th century. Like many New Englanders, he chose to have a likeness taken for posterity, and his, in symbolically depicting his disregard for society's rules, offers a very personal statement of character.

[1] The children of Stephen and Charlotte were Abigail (b. 1785), Charles (b. 1790), Chauncey (b. 1792), Francis Bushnell (b. 1796), William (b. 1799), and Benjamin (b. 1802)—the three eldest died in infancy; New Canaan, Conn., Deeds, Stephen Fitch to Ebenezer Bishop, 20 February 1810, 3: 782-784.

[2] Connecticut Archives, Lotteries and Divorces, second series, Volume One: Ackley-Parmele, Petition of Charlotte Fitch, 22 September 1807.

[3] Gerard C. Wertkin, "Zion on Clapboard Hill: The New Canaan Shakers, 1810-1812," *The New Canaan Historical Society Annual*, VIII (1979-1980): 8.

[4] Journal, Eldress Esther Bennett, Western Reserve Historical Society, Cleveland, Ohio, 13 September 1809, Shaker Records, V: B-74.

[5] Agreements signed 20 February 1810 and 2 October 1810, Records Kept by Order of the Church (Shaker), Record Book No. 2, 4-6, Shaker Record Group Collection, Rare Books and Manuscripts Division, The New York Public Library, Astor, Lenox and Tilden Foundations; see also New Canaan Deeds, 3: 782-784.

[6] Journal, Elder Nicholas Bennett, 5 March 1810, Shaker Records, NYPL; for a detailed account of the Shaker experiment in New Canaan see Wertkin, "Zion on Clapboard Hill," 6-19.

[7] Nicholas Bennett Journal, 6 June, 27 July, and 30 August 1810, Shaker Records, NYPL.

[8] Elder Daniel Goodrich to Deacon Richard Spier, 10 June 1811, Shaker Records, WRHS, IV: A-32.

[9] Goodrich to Spier, 10 June 1811; Nicholas Bennett Journal, 5 February 1811.

[10] Nicholas Bennett Journal, 8 May 1811.

[11] Esther Bennett Journal, 12 May 1811; Francis Bushnell Fitch signed the Covenant of the Second Family, New Lebanon, N.Y., on 25 February 1815, and resided among the Shakers until 19 April 1817. His grandmother, Abigail Fitch, lived at New Lebanon until her death in 1812.

[12] New Canaan Conn. Deeds, Town Hall, New Canaan, Richard Spier and Daniel Goodrich to Jacob Selleck, 2 April 1812, 2: 713.

[13] Roscoe Conkling Fitch, comp., *History of the Fitch Family A.D. 1400-1930*, I (published privately, nd) 149-150; Marshall H. Montgomery, "Shakers and Soldiers," *New Canaan Historical Society Annual* (June 1956): 111.

[14] Stephen Fitch to Benjamin Fitch, 5 April 1824, quoted in Montgomery, "Shakers and Soldiers," 111.

29.
ELISHA FREEMAN JR. (1781-1852)
Erastus Salisbury Field (1805-1900)
Lee, Mass., c. 1836
Oil on canvas
33 x 25 (83.8 x 63.5)
Old Sturbridge Village

ELISHA FREEMAN IS SEATED in a fancy chair, facing slightly to the right and directly engaging the viewer. This composition was favored by Erastus

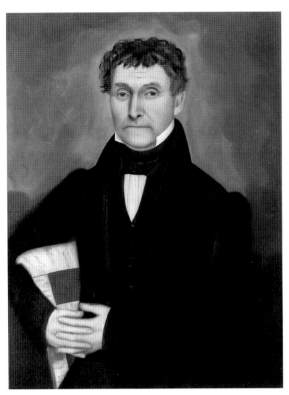

Cat. 29

Salisbury Field, and is nearly identical to his paintings of Joseph and Nathaniel Bassett (cats. 13, 15), whose likenesses he also took during his 1836 visit to Lee. Freeman was part of the Bassetts's social and kinship network, which Field exploited on his trip through the Berkshires.

Like the Bassetts, the Freeman family was among the "Cape settlers" who went to Lee in the late 1770s from Sandwich, Mass.[1] Elisha Freeman, Jr., was a member of the first generation born in the western Massachusetts town. In 1805 he married Nancy, the daughter of Cornelius Bassett, who was a cousin of Nathaniel's and also among the first residents of Lee.[2] Elisha and Nancy had five children together prior to her death in 1826. When he sat for his portrait Freeman was twice widowed, having lost his second wife, Rebecca Goodspeed, in 1833, after five years of marriage.[3]

Field's commission from Freeman almost certainly came as a result of the prosperous farmer's connection with the Bassetts. They were linked by marriage and through community associations such as the Congregational Church. Freeman witnessed several of Nathaniel Bassett's deeds, and when Elisha Freeman

died in 1852, Amos Geer Hulbert (fig. 14), another in-law, was appointed executor to administer his estate—appraised two years earlier at $7,500.[4]

[1] *History of Berkshire County, Mass., with Biographical Sketches of its Prominent Men*, II (New York: J.B. Beers & Co., 1885), 127, 129.
[2] *Bassett Genealogy*, unpublished manuscript, private collection.
[3] *V.R.*, Lee, 114, 134, 198.
[4] Berkshire County, Mass., Deeds, Courthouse, Pittsfield land transactions for Nathaniel Bassett 1810-1817; *Records of the Town of Lee From its Incorporation to A.D. 1801* (Lee, Mass.: Press of the Valley Gleaner, 1900); Berkshire County, Probate, docket #7724; Population Schedules, Lee, Mass., U.S. Census, 1850, 306: 52 (microfilm).

30.
SABRA FRIZLE (1793-1847)
Justin Salisbury
Leyden, Mass., 1828
Cut paper
3 1/4 x 3 1/4 (8.3 x 8.3)
Inscribed verso: *Sabra Frizle of Leyden February 23, 1828 Age 34 years, 8 months.*
Old Sturbridge Village

31.
RUFUS FRIZLE (1793-?)
Justin Salisbury
Leyden, Mass., 1828
Cut paper
3 3/16 x 3 3/16 (8.1 x 8.1)
Inscribed verso: *Rufus Frizle of Leyden February 23, 1828 aged 34 years & four months.*
Old Sturbridge Village

Cat. 32

32.
ALLEN FRIZLE (1826-?)
Justin Salisbury
Leyden, Mass., 1830
Cut paper
3 1/4 x 3 1/4 (8.3 x 8.3)
Inscribed verso: *Allen R. Frizzle/ Leyden Jan. 30th 1830/ Aged 4 years.*
Old Sturbridge Village

THE LEVELS OF SKILL possessed by profile artists ranged widely. Mechanical aids such as a physiognotrace or profile box were often used to trace profiles, speeding the process and increasing accuracy. The use of a pantographic device is usually revealed by an incised or graphite line bordering the edge of a profile. These three profiles bear no such marks, indicating that they were cut freehand. The artist's deftness is evident in such fine details as Sabra Frizle's hair comb and ruffled collar.

The Frizle profiles bear many hallmarks of Justin Salisbury's work. A Vermont resident, Salisbury worked primarily in the Connecticut River valley, and many of his hollow-cut silhouettes survive. His work is often embellished with pencilled details, such as the hairstyles added to Sabra and Allen Frizle's portraits. The profile of Rufus Frizle shows Salisbury's technique for defining a gentleman's clothing. He cut, in profile, the shape of the collar and coat lapels, with voids above and below defining the head and chest. Here, the coat lapels have been colored with graphite and a stock has

been drawn in ink.[1]

Attribution to Salisbury is also based on a family connection, for Justin Salisbury was married to Miranda Frizle, Rufus' younger sister.[2] Silhouette artists, like itinerant painters, used kinship networks to secure work. The Frizles, or Frizzels, were an established Leyden family. Rufus married Sabra Wells in 1820 and when they had their profiles cut, their family included two daughters and a son.[3] The couple patronized their brother-in-law on at least two occasions, as the profile of Allen was taken two years after those of his parents.

While profiles were the most inexpensive form of portraiture available, profile artists could make a reasonable living with steady work. On average, a silhouettist earned from twelve and a half to twenty-five cents for the few minutes of work required to cut a profile.[4] At those rates it was easily possible for an artist to exceed a laborer's average daily wage of one dollar. The price paid by the Frizles for their profiles would not have represented a significant investment. However, they purchased pewter frames, intended specifically for the presentation of silhouettes. The frames, which are unique to the Massachusetts-Vermont border area, have a separate pewter ring fit into the back of the frame to hold the silhouette in place. At least seven other Salisbury silhouettes are enclosed in these distinctive frames.[5]

[1] Florence Thompson Howe, "Justin Salisbury's Silhouettes," *Spinning Wheel* (March 1971): 54-55.
[2] Howe, "Salisbury's Silhouettes," 55; Rufus, the son of Reuben and

Left: Cat. 30; right: Cat. 31

Anna Frizle, was born on 2 October 1793, and his sister, Miranda was born in 1807, Vital Records of Leyden, Mass.

[3] Population Schedules, Leyden, Mass., U.S. Census, 1830, 62:100 (microfilm).

[4] On 8 April 1807, J. Fuller advertised in *The Hampshire Federal* that he charged twenty-five cents for "two correct Profiles." Mr. Brown advertised in the 25 September 1819 issue of *The Columbian Centinel* that his "price per cutting" was twelve and a half cents. Rufus Porter's 1818-20 broadside (Fig. 13, p. 37) specifies a price of twenty cents for "a common profile cut double."

[5] Howe, "Salisbury's Silhouettes," 54-55; based on geographic association these pewter frames have been attributed to the Greenfield, Mass., pewterer, Samuel Pierce, or one of his sons.

33.
FANNY NEGUS FULLER (1799-1845) AND HER SONS FRANCIS BENJAMIN (1838-1915) AND JOHN EMERY (1838-?)

Augustus Fuller (1812-1873)
Deerfield, Mass., c. 1838-1839
Oil on canvas
30" x 25" (76.2 x 63.5)
Deerfield Academy, Deerfield, Mass.
Plate 10

WRITING TO HER BROTHER in April 1824, Fanny Negus Fuller urged him to marry, but warned "its well enough to marry but you will always have to write with your child in your arms as I do now."[1] At that point in her life she had been married for four years and was already the mother of two babies and stepmother to five children ranging in age from seven to fifteen. These were the children of Aaron Fuller, a widower she had married in 1820, taking on immediately "the care & responsibility of...tender offspring."[2]

Fanny Negus Fuller wholeheartedly embraced the lifestyle of domesticity characteristic of the second quarter of the 19th century. She had experienced the independence of living and working away from home in her late teens, teaching school and sewing straw hats for a Greenfield milliner.[3] She had enjoyed the attention of several suitors, causing her brother to advise her "to shun the base desire of male embraces," and her brother-in-law to caution her "not to be too fond of walking out with gentlemen in the evening."[4] At the age of twenty-one, she accepted the proposal of the widowed Deerfield farmer, Aaron Fuller.

Settled into her own home life, Fanny took on a role in the extended Negus family network. Her father's

death in an 1816 accident had left her mother, Basmeth, to cope with eleven children.[5] Shortly after Joel Negus's death, Fanny's older sister Arathusa married and began to help their mother.[6] When Fanny married four years later, her new household in Deerfield quickly became an extension of the Petersham family circle. In 1823 Basmeth Negus "broke up keeping house" and divided her time between the homes of her two married daughters.[7] In addition to her mother, her five younger sisters also made their home with Fanny at intervals throughout the 1820s and 1830s.

The regular and lengthy visits of members of her immediate family added to the crowding and chaos in Fanny Fuller's burgeoning household. At one point she wrote home to Petersham to ask for a loan of blankets, explaining "I shall really be put to it for bedclothes this winter" with seven children and four adults in residence.[8] However, the presence of her sisters also gave Fanny  much-needed assistance with the care of her young children and with household chores such as spinning, baking, and cheese-making. As her husband wrote in 1824, "the little girls...have been quite industrious this winter, while they went to school one of them helped me about [the] house and the other braided straw."[9]

Cat. 33; photograph by Chuck Kidd

During the 1830s, Aaron Fuller became involved in various forms of entrepreneurial agriculture that took him away from home for weeks at a time. While her husband drove cattle to the Brighton livestock market, Fanny Fuller had total charge of their household and relied on her sisters for companionship and assistance. As her younger sisters married and set up homes of their own, Fanny was able to look to them for the same kind of help she had provided her mother. When Aaron Fuller was away, one or several of the children often went to stay with their aunts, freeing Fanny to take on her husband's responsibilities of running the farm, collecting debts, and transacting business in town.[10]

As they became old enough, some of the Fuller children went away to school. The first to go were

Aaron and Augustus (see cats. 24, 25), Aaron Fuller's two oldest children from his first marriage, both of whom were deaf. In 1824, at the age of twelve, Augustus was enrolled at the American Asylum for the Education and Instruction of Deaf and Dumb Persons.[11] He lived at the Asylum in Hartford for five years and wrote his parents that he studied painting and would "carry some pretty pictures home."[12] Upon leaving the school he commenced his career as an itinerant artist, returning to Deerfield for occasional visits. Fanny Fuller monitored her stepson's progress in her letters, writing to her husband "we all wish verry [sic] much to see [Augustus] we hear he paints fine."[13] On visits home he often took likenesses of family and neighbors (see cats. 34, 45, 79), including this portrait of his stepmother and his infant brothers.

Not long after the birth of the twins, the last of her seven children, Fanny's health began to fail. She was afflicted with pulmonary tuberculosis, and by 1844 was a complete invalid. By that time, all but the youngest of her children had left home, and she wrote her sisters that she missed the bustle of family life and the routine of household chores. As she explained to Arathusa, "I do not sit up more than half the day and am intirely unable to work...I have got poor Aaron to fix for winter, and then I must give up. We expect a lonesome Thanksgiving as the boys cannot afford to come home."[14] Her debilitating illness brought a longing for the former fullness of her life and she wrote of her difficulty trying "to wean" herself "from this world and prepare...for the world of spirits."[15]

Fanny Fuller's frustration with the changes in her daily routine reveals the fulfillment she had found as a wife and mother. Her portrait provides a lasting image of her love for and commitment to her children. Throughout her life she was an integral part of an extensive family network, working to sustain it and drawing on its resources. The rhythms and responsibilities of Fanny Fuller's life echo those of many New England women, but she, unlike most women, left both written and visual documentation of the richness of her life.

[1] Fanny Fuller to Nathan Negus, 18 April 1824, Fuller/Negus Papers.
[2] Fanny Fuller to Aaron Fuller, 15 June c.1833, Fuller/Negus Papers.
[3] See letters: Joseph Negus to Fanny Negus, 13 April 1818, Fuller/Negus Papers, "when you write please let me know whether you have a Ladies School in Petersham this summer."; Luthera Negus to Nathan Negus, 19 May 1820, collection of Petersham Historical Society, "Fanny has gone to Greenfield to spend a few weeks with a Mrs. Stanhope and sew straw."; Fanny Negus to Nathan Negus, 30 August 1817, Fuller/Negus Papers, "I have sewed you a handsome straw hat."
[4] Nathan Negus to Fanny Negus, 31 January 1819; Jonas Howe to Fanny Negus, 27 June 1820, Fuller/Negus Papers.
[5] J.B. Howe, Sketches of Petersham Natives and Adopted Citizens (1915), 40.
[6] Vital Records of Petersham, Mass., to the end of the Year 1849 (Worcester, 1904), 126, 183. See also, Fuller/Negus Papers.
[7] Fanny Fuller to Nathan Negus, 18 April 1824.
[8] Fanny Fuller to Arathusa Howe, 12 October 1823, Fuller/Negus Papers.
[9] Aaron Fuller to Nathan Negus, 18 April 1824, Fuller/Negus Papers.
[10] Fanny Fuller to Aaron Fuller, 31 May and 15 June c. 1833, Fuller/Negus Papers.
[11] Luthera Negus to Nathan Negus, 4 October 1824, Petersham Historical Society: "I calculate to go to D. to assist in fixing Aaron & Augustus off to the Asylum, they are to go the last of this month."; Tenth Report of the Directors of the American, 26; Eleventh Report (1827), 31; Twelfth Report (1828), 6.
[12] Augustus Fuller to Aaron Fuller, 4 August 1828, Fuller-Higginson Papers, box 5, folder 6.
[13] Fanny Fuller to Aaron Fuller, 31 May c. 1833.
[14] Fanny Fuller to Arathusa Howe, 10 November c. 1844, Fuller/Negus Papers.
[15] Fanny Fuller to Laura Negus Spooner, c. August/September 1844, Fuller /Negus Papers.

34.

MERCY BEMIS FULLER (1763-1841)
Augustus Fuller (1812-1873)
Deerfield or Fitchburg, Mass., c. 1831-1841
Watercolor on paper
3 1/8 x 2 1/4
Inscribed verso: *Mercy Bemis Fuller/ Sketched by her Grandson/ Augustus Fuller/ born 1763 – / died Jan.[y] 29, 1842.*
Pocumtuck Valley Memorial Association,
Memorial Hall Museum, Deerfield, Mass.

AUGUSTUS FULLER'S DETERMINATION to lead an independent life as a painter was a matter of deep concern to his parents and siblings. Their fear for his safety when he traveled alone was based on his deafness and his bouts of alcoholism. "My Dear Brother George," wrote the artist's sister Harriet:

[Augustus] is going to leave home...I dislike to have him go but he says he shall look out, and not get into bad company, he has said the same before, and I feel afraid to trust him again away from home. Father has talked with him... but I do not think he could be persuaded to give up the idea of going, as he has nothing to do at home now, and he thinks he could be earning a little money.[1]

The family network, extending from Deerfield across central Massachusetts to Boston, functioned as a safety net for the artist. The Fullers kept careful track of his movements, and members of the family sometimes traveled with Augustus or provided him with lodgings. An important part of this network was the branch of the family in Fitchburg, the home of Augustus's grandparents, Azariah and Mercy Fuller, and several of their twelve children.

It is likely that Fuller painted this miniature portrait of his grandmother on one of his visits to Fitchburg. The style of her clothing suggests that the likeness was taken in the early 1830s, when she was in her seventies and Augustus was beginning his work as an itinerant painter. The hesitancy of a young artist is evident in the reworking of the top of Mrs. Fuller's cap and the blocky composition of the portrait. These elements and the small slip of paper on which the image is painted impart a feeling of intimacy and informality.

[1] Harriet P. Fuller to George Fuller, 14 December 1851, Fuller/Negus Papers.

Cat. 34; photograph by Chuck Kidd

35.
MARY B. GODDARD (1806-?)
Horace Bundy (1814-1883)
Nashua, N.H., 1837
Oil on canvas
28 x 26 (71.1 x 66)
Inscribed verso: *Mary B. Goddard/ AE 31/ By H. Bundy/ Sept 1837*
Heritage Plantation of Sandwich, Sandwich, Mass.

36.
NATHAN W. GODDARD (1800-?)
Horace Bundy (1814-1883)
Nashua, N.H., 1837
Oil on canvas
28 x 26 (71.1 x 66)
Inscribed verso: *N. W. Goddard/ AE 37/ By H. Bundy/ Sept 1837*
Heritage Plantation of Sandwich, Sandwich, Mass.

37.
FRANKLIN W. GODDARD
(1833-before 1850)
Horace Bundy (1814-1883)
Nashua, N.H., 1837
Oil on canvas
28 x 23 15/16 (71.1 x 60.8)
Inscribed verso: *Franklin W. Godard/ Agd 4 years/ Nashua 1837*
Old Sturbridge Village

38.
JOHN M. GODDARD (1831-?)
Horace Bundy (1814-1883)
Nashua, N.H., 1837
Oil on canvas
28 1/8 x 24 13/16 (71.4 x 63)
Inscribed verso: *John M. Goddard/ Agd 6 years/ Nashua 1837*
Old Sturbridge Village

THE SIGNED AND DATED Goddard family portraits are among the earliest documented examples of the work of Horace Bundy and illustrate the anatomical distortion that is characteristic of his first efforts at portraiture. The notations in large black script on the backs of these canvases are also a trademark of Bundy's. When these portraits were painted the twenty-three-

year-old artist had not yet codified some of the compositional devices seen in his later work, such as framing his subjects in a painted oval or setting them against landscapes.[1]

Throughout his career as an itinerant artist, which extended at least through the 1850s, Bundy worked primarily in his home region of Vermont and New Hampshire, creating a visual record of tradesmen and their families (see cat. 48). Nathan and Mary Goddard had both been born in Connecticut, but were living in Nashua, N.H., by 1831 when John, the first of their six children, was born.[2] When the portraits were painted in 1837, the Goddards were the parents of three sons, but it is not known if a likeness was taken of one-year-old Nathan William.

For the special occasion of their portrait sitting, John and Franklin were dressed in matching outfits. Their identical rust frock coats and broad collared shirts bespeak their fraternity as much as any physical resemblance. The objects held by the boys indicate that they are at different developmental stages. John, who is six, holds a primer, showing that he is already attending school and learning to read. The hammer clasped in Franklin's hand suggests the four-year-old's developing manual dexterity.

Similarly, Nathan Goddard's tools signify his occupation. The left-handed craftsman is in the process of repairing a watch, illustrating the work done by American watchmakers.[3] Goddard advertised himself as a "Dealer in Gold and Silver Watches" from the "best manufactories in Switzerland and England," who "repaired and warranted" watches and clocks.[4] In 1851, Goddard's store was described as "a large and commodious concern, well filled with a large and splendid assortment of all articles usually kept in a Jeweller's Store."[5] These included silver spoons, pen knives, scissors, and jewelry. The ring, brooch, gold beads, and earrings adorning Mary Goddard were probably selected from among the "gold beads" and "assortment of Jewelry" in her husband's store.[6]

Top: Cat. 35; below: Cat. 37; Opposite top: Cat. 36; Opposite below: Cat. 38

[1] John and Katherine Ebert, *American Folk Painters* (New York: Charles Scribner's Sons, 1975), 57.
[2] Population Schedules, Nashua, N.H, U.S. Census, 1850, 434: 253 (microfilm).
[3] Chris H. Bailey, *Two Hundred Years of American Clocks & Watches* (Englewood Cliffs, N.J.: Prentice-Hall, Inc. and Rutledge Books), 191.
[4] John Sawtell, *The Nashua Directory* (Nashua, 1841), 9; *The Farmers' Guide, A Description of the Business of Nashua and Nashville* (Nashua: Kimball & Dodge, 1851), 30.

[5] *Farmers' Guide*, 30.
[6] Sawtell, *Nashua Directory*, 9.

39.
EDWARD W. GORHAM (1842-1844)
Joseph Whiting Stock (1815-1855)
Springfield, Mass., 1844
Oil on canvas
30 1/8 x 25 (76.5 x 63.5)
Inscribed verso: *Feb. 19th 1844 died / Aged 1 yr. 8 mo. 2 da./ Painted by J.W. Stock / Springfield, Mass*
New York State Historical Association, Cooperstown, N.Y.
Plate 12

"WHAT WOULD WE NOT GIVE, in some circumstances, for a good portrait of a departed friend?"[1] This question, posed in a fictional account of a boy's quest for an image of his deceased sister, guided hundreds of early-19th-century New Englanders who commissioned memorial portraits. Taking likenesses after death was a regular part of the business of artist Joseph Whiting Stock. Among his paintings of children, roughly one out of every five was a posthumous portrait.[2] This figure, which is more than twenty times greater than the occurrences of Stock's paintings of adults after death, bears testimony to the fact that, while child mortality rates dropped in the 19th century, at least one child in a family usually did not reach adulthood. It also reflects the particular sorrow of losing a child who, because of the brevity of his or her life, left no mark.

Yet there is little in this image of a toddler playfully hammering tacks to indicate that it is a posthumous portrait. That information is provided by the memorial inscription on the reverse, which gives the child's precise age and the date of his death. The subject has been identified as Edward W. Gorham, the son of Joseph W. and Laura N. Rogers Gorham of Springfield, Mass., who died on 19 February 1844, the date recorded on the painting.[3] An 1844 entry in Stock's journal notes that he painted "J.W. Gorham's boy deceased" on a canvas that measured 30" by 25."[4] The artist's accounts show that he was paid $12 for his work. Around the same time Stock also painted three other Springfield boys who had died.

Cat. 39

Stock's journal entries merely indicate when a painting's subject was "deceased" or "dead." Isaac Augustus Wetherby, a painter for whom posthumous portraits comprised fifteen percent of his output, made more detailed notations about his subjects. Usually summoned to paint a portrait "after death from corpse," he also took likenesses of people near death. His account book records painting portraits of people "on their sick bed" or "in the last stage of consumption." Wetherby's description of taking a portrait "from corps and recolection" underscores the difficulty of creating a posthumous image that captured its subject's appearance in life. For many artists, the invention of photography simplified this frustrating and unpleasant task, and within a few years Wetherby's post-mortem portraits were described as "after death from Daguerreotype."[5]

[1] *New England Farmer*, VII (November, 1858), 502.
[2] Jack Larkin's analysis of the data in *The Paintings and the Journal of Joseph Whiting Stock*, ed. Juliette Tomlinson (Middletown, Conn.: Wesleyan University Press, 1976).
[3] Paul S. D'Ambrosio and Charlotte M. Emans, *Folk Art's Many Faces, Portraits in the New York State Historical Association* (Cooperstown, NY: New York State Historical Association, 1987): 143.
[4] *Journal of Joseph Whiting Stock*, 41.
[5] Ploog, "Account Books of I.A. Wetherby," 78.

40.
MRS. MOSES GREEN
Ruth Henshaw Bascom (1772-1848)
Ashby, Mass., before 1831
Pastel on paper
19 x 14 1/8 (48.3 x 35.9)
Old Sturbridge Village
Plate 22

Left: Cat. 40; right: Cat. 41

41.
MOSES GREEN
Ruth Henshaw Bascom (1772-1848)
Ashby, Mass., before 1831
Pastel on paper
19 1/16 x 14 13/16 (48.4 x 37.6)
Old Sturbridge Village
Plate 23

THROUGHOUT HER CAREER as a profile artist, Ruth Henshaw Bascom (cat. 11) worked within an extended network of family and friends. The subjects of these portraits, Mr. and Mrs. Moses Green, were neighbors of the Reverend and Mrs. Bascom during their residence in Ashby, Mass., from 1820 to 1839. In her journal Bascom recorded regular social encounters with the Greens, as when she mentioned "Mr. Moses Green...called in evening," or "Mr. Bascom to Mr. Moses Green's & dined there."[1]

The style of these portraits suggests a date after 1828, when Bascom began coloring her profiles with crayons.[2] They were definitely executed before 1831, when Bascom improved and reframed her likenesses of the Greens.[3] In the same period she also took a posthumous profile of the Greens' daughter, Mrs. Mary Green Taylor, who died in 1829 at the age of twenty-four. During Mrs. Taylor's final illness, Bascom recorded regular ministerial visits by her husband to the Greens. On 24 December 1829, the day after Mary Taylor's death, the Bascoms rode together to the Greens, where Ruth "took the outlines of Mrs. Taylor's features (in her shroud) while Mr. Bascom & the family made arrangements for the funeral." Later that afternoon she began "to paint" the portrait.[4]

The phrase "took the outlines" seems to describe a process of actually tracing a subject's profile. Little is known about Bascom's technique, but she may have used a system similar to a physiognotrace, by which a profile was traced from a cast shadow. Indeed, she described her works as "shadows," and on two occasions noted darkening a room to take a profile.[5]

After Bascom had drawn a silhouette, she usually cut it out. The life-size scale of her portrait busts is uncommon in the tradition of New England cut-paper profiles. In her mature work, the last phase of creating a likeness was to "paint" colored details onto the profile using pastel crayons. Many of her portraits have additional details made of applied paper (see cat. 55). The Greens's silhouettes are actually constructed of two parts; on each the face and neck are overlaid with a profile of the clothing. In Mr. Green's silhouette this is an especially effective device, for the slight shadow cast by the separate collar heightens the realism of the image.

[1] Ruth Henshaw Bascom Diaries, 2 October and 23 December 1829.
[2] Ruth Henshaw Bascom Diaries, 14 January 1828 notes taking "a likeness in crayons, the first I have done in this Town."
[3] Ruth Henshaw Bascom Diaries, entry of 1831.
[4] Ruth Henshaw Bascom Diaries, entries of 9 December to 25 December 1829.
[5] Fouratt, "Ruth Henshaw Bascom," 197.

42.
JESSE HARTSHORN (1813-1889)
William Matthew Prior (1806-1873)
Portland, Me., 1836
Oil on cardboard
24 7/16 x 20 15/16 (62 x 53.2)
Inscribed verso: *Mr. Jesse Hartshorn / Painted from Nature/ By Wm M Prior Feby 24 1836 / Portland Maine*
Old Sturbridge Village

43.
LUCY A. HARTSHORN
William Matthew Prior (1806-1873)
Portland, Me., 1836
Oil on cardboard
24 11/16 x 21 7/16 (62.7 x 54.5)
Inscribed verso: *Mrs. Hartshorn/ Painted from Nature by/ Wm M Prior. Portland Feby 24 1836*
Old Sturbridge Village

WILLIAM MATTHEW PRIOR is renowned for the artistic versatility seen in the stylistic variety of his work, which ranges from crude and flat to sophisticated and painterly (see cats. 53, 54, 57, 80). The Hartshorn portraits exemplify Prior's more academic style, with deft handling of light, shadow, color, and volume, and lifelike rendering of skin tone and anatomy. Lucy Hartshorn's portrait has a particular immediacy as she appears to turn slightly to engage the viewer directly.

That works as disparate as these and Prior's less developed portraits came from the same painter's hand belies the notion that all non-academic artists worked in a naive style because they lacked ability. Even Prior's earliest works demonstrate real talent, as in his accomplished self-portrait (pl. 4), painted in 1825 when he was nineteen years old. When that mature artwork was created, Prior was working as an ornamental painter in his home community of Bath, Me.[1] The young artisan-painter's advertisements show his efforts to attract a broad market by providing a range of competitively priced services. There is compelling evidence that the quality of his work was in direct proportion to the price paid for it. Prior developed a price scale for portraits that equated cost with the time spent on a likeness and the difficulty of its composition. He evolved this

Cat. 42

system early in his career, for even in his first advertisement as a portrait painter he noted that reduced rates were available for "side views and profiles of children."[2] By 1831, Prior was more specific, offering "a likeness without shade or shadow at one quarter price."[3]

The portraits of Jesse and Lucy Hartshorn have "shade" and "shadow", or modelling. The artist advertised that such fully realized portraits cost ten to twenty-five dollars, or four times the price of his

much larger than the other".[6]

[1] For example, Prior advertised: "ornamental painting, old tea trays, waiters re-jappaned and ornamented in very tasty style. Bronzing, oil guilding and varnishing by Wm. M. Prior, Bath. No. 1 Middle Street," *Maine Inquirer*, 5 June 1827 .
[2] *Maine Inquirer*, 28 February 1828.
[3] *Maine Inquirer*, 5 April 1831.
[4] *Maine Inquirer*, 1830.
[5] The son of William J. and Abigail Hartshorn, in 1850 Jesse was listed as a joiner. Population Schedules, Portland, Me., U.S. Census, 1850, 252: 232 (microfilm).
[6] Nathaniel Hawthorne, *The American Notebooks* (New Haven: Yale University Press, 1932), 61.

44.
NATHANAEL HOWE (1764-1837)
Zedekiah Belknap (1781-1858)
Hopkinton, Mass., c. 1815
Oil on panel
27 1/4 x 22 1/2 (69.2 x 57.1)
Old Sturbridge Village

THE WOOD PANEL ON WHICH the Reverend Nathanael Howe's likeness is painted has been subtly textured with diagonal lines to resemble canvas twill, a trademark of Zedekiah Belknap (cats. 27, 51, 52). The grayish sizing on the back of this painting is also a feature of the artist's technique.[1] Belknap, who briefly studied divinity at Dartmouth College, painted several ministers' portraits. In the 18th century, clergymen were often memorialized by a likeness, but by Belknap's period of activity, 1810-1848, this practice had become less common. Not surprisingly, most of Belknap's ministerial likenesses date to his early career, while the bulk of his work, like that of his peers, concentrated on prospering professionals, farmers, and mechanics.

Howe's tenure as minister of the First Congregational Church of Hopkinton, Mass., extended from 1791-1837. His relationship with his parish was more in keeping with 18th-century ministerial practice than the egalitarian approach that was the norm in the 1830s. The earlier tradition is reflected in Howe's training, his dress, his occupation as a farmer-minister, and in his authoritarian relationship with his congregation. A clergyman of a younger generation remembered that when Howe spoke on "any subject of interest, his eye would kindle and his features express great vivacity of thought and emotion." Above

Cat. 43   cheapest flat pictures.[4] When the Hartshorns sat for Prior he was working in Portland, Me., where he maintained a studio for several years in the 1830s.

The Hartshorns' prosperity is evident in their decision to commission Prior's best quality paintings and in their demeanor and accoutrements. This fashionable couple expressed their participation in polite society through their clothing and deportment. Lucy Hartshorn's formal black decolleté dress with an elaborately folded bodice, her elegant drop earrings, and the paisley shawl draped over her chair, all reveal a woman of taste and refinement. Her attire and relaxed and welcoming expression suggest someone waiting to receive callers or prepared for an evening entertainment. These confident social signals are somewhat surprising, as the paintings depict a newly married artisan and his wife, both in their early twenties. Jesse Hartshorn was the son of a joiner, and throughout his life worked as a joiner and carpenter.[5] The portrait, however, shows him in his best suit of clothes. The only hint at his occupation is his muscular right hand, at the center of the painting's composition. This calls to mind Hawthorne's description of a blacksmith, recognized "because his right hand was all, however, he was "remembered and spoken of as a man of marked individuality and great eccentricity."[2]

Born in Ipswich, Mass., in 1764, Howe was educated at two universities (Princeton and Harvard) and by study with four clergymen. The last was the Reverend Nathaniel Emmons of Franklin, Mass., whom he greatly admired and with whom he remained in close contact throughout his life. Howe appears to have emulated his mentor in matters of dress. For the portrait, he wore the old-fashioned ministerial garb of a robe and white bands. Worn since the days of John Calvin, the Geneva gown and linen bands had long been the traditional symbols of the Congregational minister's authority. Howe's teacher, Dr. Emmons, was remembered as "defending the bands and cocked hats," reflecting his opinion that "clergymen, when they travel or go abroad, should have some badge of their profession. It preserves them from any unpleasant encounters and causes them to remember their sacred office."[3]

Howe was among the last to follow this practice, which by 1820 was unusual enough to elicit comment. A reminiscence of life in central Massachusetts described a minister, "near middle age," who:

> wore his black silk gown not only in the pulpit but (in summer time) in making pastoral calls. He was the last of Quabbin's ministers to wear it, and much of the stately grace of the olden time went out with its flowing sleeves.[4]

Howe doubtless provided his Hopkinton parishioners with similar memories.

Howe's account of his tenure, presented near the midpoint of his career at an anniversary of the church, offers a glimpse into his pastoral relationship with his congregation. In his "Century Sermon," preached in 1815, he reviewed the history of Hopkinton and its church, his own call to the ministry, and his theology. He also used the forum of the centennial to remind his people that his annual salary, established at $233.33 at the time of his settlement, had never been changed and had been paid irregularly. By his own estimation, Howe spent more of his time farming than in ministry. "Borne down with the fatigues of manual labor, pressed into the woods in the winter, to the plough in the spring, and into the meadow in the summer, to support my family comfortably, and fulfil my promises, I felt the business of the ministry has been greatly neglected," he wrote. "It was impossible for me to do what ought to be done in my profession, unless the people did more toward my support." He went on to ask, "do you know by what means I have become so rich, as to have a great house, finished and furnished; a farm, a herd of cattle, a flock of sheep, horses, and money at interest?" His answer was decisive and not flattering: "because I have been doing your business and neglecting my own." Their business, he pointed out, was "to support your minister," and his was "to study and preach."[5] The chastising tone of the sermon shows Howe's confidence in his authority.

Shortly after this sermon was preached the congregation gave Howe a new surplice and "an elegant suit of clothes," for which he thanked them in a published edition of the sermon. He also thanked "those who have paid kind attention to our daughter Eliza during her two-year illness."[6] (Eliza, the second of four children borne by Howe's wife, Olive Jones, had died soon after the sermon had been delivered.) As a further expression of their esteem, the congregation may have commissioned this portrait of Howe and the companion painting of his wife. The pictures

Cat. 44

belonged to the First Congregational Church of Hopkinton until they were consigned to auction in 1981.

[CS]

[1] The companion portrait of Olive Jones Howe, with similar characteristics, is in the Old Sturbridge Village collection. See Mankin, "Zedekiah Belknap," 1056-7.

[2] William B. Sprague, "Nathanael Howe, 1790-1837," *Annals of the American Pulpit*, II (New York: Robert Carter and Brothers, 1859), 308-9.

[3] Edward A. Park, *Memoir of Nathaniel Emmons with Sketches of his Friends and Pupils* (Boston: Congregational Board of Publications, 1861), 157, 127.

[3] Francis H. Underwood, *Quabbin, the Story of a Small Town with Outlooks Upon Puritan Life* (London, 1893), 41.

[4] Nathanael Howe, *A Century Sermon delivered in Hopkinton, Mass., on Lord's Day, December 24, 1815*, Second ed., (Andover: Flagg and Gould, 1817), 20, 25-26.

[5] Howe, *Century Sermon*, 27.

Cat. 45

45.

ELIHU HOYT (1771-1833)

Augustus Fuller (1812-1873)
Deerfield, Mass., c. 1830
Oil on wood panel
24 x 17 5/8 (61 x 44.9)
Drawn verso: a sketch of a woman wearing a turban
Pocumtuck Valley Memorial Association, Memorial Hall Museum, Deerfield, Mass.

ELIHU HOYT WAS DESCRIBED as "an important man in his generation." Born to an established Deerfield family, he was known for his service as a colonel of the militia in the war of 1812 and as a longtime representative of his community in state and local politics.[1] He was an articulate and literate man, who documented his life in a series of journals and published a brief history of Deerfield in 1833.[2]

Hoyt was a farmer, as were most of the residents of Deerfield, and he was one of the founders of the Franklin Agricultural Society. He lived in a time and place in which agriculture became increasingly market oriented, and Hoyt struggled to adapt to the changing environment. His primary crops were oats and peas, which he sold as feed to other area farmers raising stall-fed cattle. However, he did not have enough land for commercial farming and was beset by problems that precluded successful competition in the marketplace.[3] When Hoyt died in 1833, his property had to be sold to pay his debts.[4]

Hoyt enjoyed success in his political career, which began at the local level as a selectman, justice of the peace, and member of the board of assessors. In 1803, at the age of thirty-two, Hoyt was elected to the state legislature. For twenty-seven of the next thirty years he served as a representative or senator in the Massachusetts General Court, and in 1820 he represented Deerfield at a constitutional convention.[5] A conservative Federalist, Hoyt's experience as a farmer made him an effective advocate for the agrarian interests of his constituents.

As Deerfield's representative, Hoyt also championed the cause of Augustus Fuller (cats. 24, 25, 33, 34, 77, 79). In 1826, two years after Augustus joined his older brother Aaron at the American Asylum for the Deaf and Dumb, his father could no longer afford the annual tuition of $115;[6] Hoyt successfully petitioned the Massachusetts Legislature on their behalf for state support.

Enclosed you will find the Governour certificate for your son Augustus to remain at the Hartford Asylum, the resolve on which this certificate is predicated, passed in consequence of the petition you signed when here this winter. Mr. Winship has interested himself very much in this business...I hope the little fellows will improve their priviledges & succeed in their education to the extent of our most sanguine expectations.[7]

Hoyt was evidently known to have had an interest in the arts, for in 1820, Augustus Fuller's stepmother, Fanny (cat. 33), had endeavored to secure a commission from Hoyt for her brother Nathan Negus (cat. 59), to whom she wrote:

Gen Hoyt of Deerfield thinks he should like to have his family miniatures painted ...you will find Gen Hoyt a good judge of painting he is a man of good information you will like to converse with him.[8]

Fanny may also have been involved in arranging for her stepson to take Hoyt's likeness. Or perhaps this portrait was painted as a form of thanks after Augustus Fuller left the Asylum in 1828.

[1] George Sheldon, *A History of Deerfield, Mass.* (Deerfield, 1895), 216.
[2] Hoyt Family Papers, Box 6 folder 2, Pocumtuck Valley Memorial Association Library, Deerfield, Mass.; Elihu Hoyt, *A Brief Sketch of the First Settlement of Deerfield, Mass.* (Greenfield, MA: James P. Fogg, 1833).
[3] John Wills, "Federalists are Poor Losers: Elihu Hoyt at the 1820 Massachusetts Constitutional Convention," unpublished manuscript, PVMA Library, (1982): 1.
[4] Most of Hoyt's property was purchased by his son Henry King Hoyt (1810-1863), see Franklin County, Mass., Probate Records, Courthouse, Greenfield, Docket #7283.
[5] Wills, "Federalists are Poor Losers," 5; Sheldon, *History of Deerfield,* 216.
[6] *Tenth Report of the Directors of the American Asylum* (1826).
[7] Elihu Hoyt to Aaron Fuller, 20 February 1826, Fuller-Higginson Papers, Box 1, Folder 4.
[8] Fanny Negus to Nathan Negus, 30 July 1820, Fuller/Negus Papers.

46.
SARAH PUFFER HUBBARD (1815-1889)
Robert Peckham (1785-1877)
Probably Westminster, Mass., c. 1842
Oil on canvas
29 x 24 (73.7 x 61)
Old Sturbridge Village

47.   *Cat. 46*
NEWTON SIMEON HUBBARD
(1816-1897)
Robert Peckham (1785-1877)
Probably Westminster, Mass., c. 1842
Oil on canvas
29 x 24 (73.7 x 61)
Inscribed verso: *Peckham*
Old Sturbridge Village

IN SEPTEMBER 1842, Newton Hubbard of Brimfield, Mass., traveled north to Westminster to marry Sarah Puffer.[1] It was presumably then that the couple commissioned Robert Peckham (cat. 26), also a resident of Westminster, to paint their portraits. Sittings often coincided with important life transitions, commemorating events such as marriage. The Hubbards' clothing, which corroborates the 1842 date, is so stylish that these portraits may well have been acquired for the wedding.

Newton and Sarah were both teachers, a shared vocation that may have led to their acquaintance. A native of Brimfield, Newton began his education in a district school, followed by study at Monson and Westfield academies. Less is known about Sarah's background. As one of ten children, there may have been a strong economic need for her to seek the independence afforded by teaching. Family history recalls that she was the daughter of "a woman of uncommon mind," a trait Sarah was said to share.[2]

Following their marriage the couple settled in the Hubbard family home in Brimfield, which Newton would eventually inherit.[3] Their first daughter, Mary, was born in 1844, followed by another daughter, Sarah, and a son, John. Late in life, Mary Hubbard Ormes offered this glimpse of the Sunday routine in the Hubbard household: "after dinner, we read religious newspapers, Sunday school books and sang religious songs. There was no visiting or pleasure riding."[4]

By mid-century Newton Hubbard had become active in town and state government. In Brimfield he was on the school committee and served as a tax assessor and selectman. He was a Hampden County commissioner and in 1863 represented Brimfield

in the Massachusetts General Court. He eventually supervised the maintenance of Brimfield's footpaths and roadways, a service for which he was paid $350 in 1876. About that time, he and Sarah sat again for a pair of portraits, this time by a photographer. The surviving pictures of a plump and very Victorian Sarah and a wrinkled and whiskered Newton offer a compelling counterpoint to their youthful portraits.[5]

[1] *V.R.*, Westminster.
[2] Mary Hubbard Ormes, "Memories of Hubbard Home on Tower Hill" (1928), Hubbard Family File, Brimfield Public Library, Brimfield, Mass.
[3] Hampden County, Mass, Registry of Probate, Hall of Records, Springfield, Case 21524, May 5, 1897.
[4] Ormes, "Memories of Hubbard Home."
[5] Hubbard Family File.

48.
SAMUEL HUMPHREY (1809-1840)
Horace Bundy (1814-1883)
St. Johnsbury, Vt., 1839
Oil on canvas
28 x 24 (71.1 x 61)
Inscribed verso: *Portrait of Samᶦ Humphrey Price $5.00/ Taken by Horace Bundy May 15ᵗʰ 1839*
Old Sturbridge Village

THE COMPOSITION OF THIS PORTRAIT echoes Bundy's portrait of Nathan Goddard (cat. 35), although here, instead of a watchmaker's tools, the objects are associated with storekeeping. The quill pen, pen knife, and sheaf of bills are offered as emblems of Samuel Humphrey's trade and proclaim that his status derived from success in business. As a merchant, Humphrey was among the most affluent and influential residents of St. Johnsbury, a fact that his portrait expresses along with his confidence in continued prosperity.

This painting of the thirty-year-old merchant quickly shifted from being an object that exalted the man to one that memorialized him. Eighteen months after his portrait sitting, Humphrey died of typhoid fever, leaving his wife of three years with the care of their sons, aged two years and six months respectively.[1] This portrait, a silver pocket watch, and the family Bible are the only artifacts associated with the merchant that have survived. Humphrey inherited the watch from his father, which suggests

Cat. 48

its value as well as strong ties between father and son. The importance of kinship to Humphrey is shown by the detailed family record maintained in the front of the Bible. Additionally, that volume speaks of a life rooted in a Christian faith that offered its adherents moral guidance as well as solace.

Although this Bundy portrait is similar to Nathan Goddard's, the artist had honed his skills in the two years between the sittings. His rendering of Humphrey is more lifelike, and he had become more adept at creating the illusion of space by mottling the background. The ingenious perspective of the table top also helps to define space while allowing the viewer to clearly see the objects arrayed on the table's surface.

The fee of five dollars paid to Bundy by Humphrey is at the low end of the prices paid to itinerant artists for full-sized oil portraits. Based on accounts of non-academic artists, the prices averaged between five and fifteen dollars, with some painters occasionally receiving as much as twenty-five dollars for a painting. Pricing was rarely consistent and seems to have been influenced as much by the complexity of a commission as by what a patron was willing to pay. As Augustus Fuller complained to his brother, in the country "cheaper

& plain work" makes "fools eyes large & wide"; in the city, he had heard, "first portraits get fifty dollars."[2]

[1] Humphrey Family *Bible*, Old Sturbridge Village Research Library.
[2] Augustus Fuller to George Fuller, April 1843 and 4 September 1842, Fuller/Negus Papers.

49.
HARRIET EVELITH KILNER (1799-?)
William Fisk Ainsworth (1808-1853)
Barre, Mass., 1839
Oil on canvas
30 x 25 (76.1 x 63.5)
Inscribed verso: *Mrs. F. Kilner. Aged 41./ Painted by W.F.Ainsworth./ Barre Mass Aug 1839.*
Old Sturbridge Village
Plate 22

50.
FREDERICK KILNER (1799-?)
William Fisk Ainsworth (1808-1853)
Barre, Mass., 1839
Oil on canvas
30 x 25 (76.1 x 63.5)
Inscribed verso: *Frederick Kilner. Aged 41./ painted by Wm F. Ainsworth./ Barre Mass Aug, 1839.*
Old Sturbridge Village
Plate 23

A TAILOR MAY BE IDENTIFIED, explained Nathaniel Hawthorne in 1838, if "his coat" has "not a single wrinkle in it."[1] This assertion is borne out by a close look at Frederick Kilner's impeccable clothing, and his occupation is confirmed by the trade journal clasped in his hand. A tailor's personal appearance was his most important advertisement to his neighbors. In an age when most clothing was still hand-sewn, rural tailors like Kilner were patronized primarily for the fabrication of garments such as fitted coats, which were difficult to construct. To increase business they promoted their special knowledge of fashion, drawing customers who wanted clothes cut in the latest styles. For example, in 1839 Kilner announced to the residents of Barre that he had "received the Fashions for the present and coming seasons."[2]

Cat. 49

Cat. 50

An English immigrant, Kilner had begun his career in the western Massachusetts town of Belchertown.[3] In 1830, he and his family relocated to Barre, where they lived and ran their business above the general store on the town common.[4] Kilner's tailoring shop was in a bustling rural village, which in 1835 supported two taverns, a hat shop, a palm leaf shop, a printing office, a book store, and miscellaneous other shops.[5] The tailoring business flourished so well that Kilner hired a journeyman to assist him in 1837, and two years later advertised for an experienced tailoress and an apprentice.[6]

It was at that point that the Kilners sat for William Fisk Ainsworth, a local artist. The couple, who had been married for nearly twenty years and were the parents of eight children, chose to be shown seated at either end of a handsome upholstered sofa. Mrs Kilner's black silk dress and decorative cap and collar, as crisp and stylish as her husband's clothes, exemplify the standards of propriety for a woman of her age, although her dark brown false curls hint at vanity. The book that she holds is a potent symbol, linked to New England's long tradition of respect for the written word. This common object speaks of her literacy and her role as an instructor to her children, guiding them in academic and moral lessons.

[1] Hawthorne, *American Notebooks*, 61.
[2] *Barre Gazette*, 3 May 1839.
[3] Population Schedules, Templeton, Mass., U.S. Census, 1850, 340: 281; Belchertown, Mass., 1820, 50:183 (microfilm).
[4] *Barre Gazette*, Souvenir Supplement, May 1897; *Barre Gazette*, 20 September 1973.
[5] "Survey of Barre Common," drawn by John King, 27 May 1835, Barre Historical Society.
[6] *Barre Gazette*, 6 October 1837; *Barre Gazette*, 3 May 1839.

51.
SUSAN MILLER KNIGHT (1796-1884)
AND ASA RANDOLPH KNIGHT
(1831-1910)
Zedekiah Belknap (1781-1858)
Dummerston, Vt., 1832
Oil on canvas
29 5/8 x 24 5/8 (75.3 x 62.6)
William D. Hamill

52.
ASA KNIGHT (1793-1851)
Zedekiah Belknap (1781-1858)
Dummerston, Vt., 1832
Oil on canvas
29 5/8 x 24 5/8 (75.3 x 62.6)
William D. Hamill

ACCORDING TO A REMINISCENCE by Asa Randolph Knight, these portraits were painted by Zedekiah Belknap in 1832, when Susan Knight was 36, her husband 39, and Asa Randolph was a year old. A line drawing of the portrait of Susan Knight and lithographs of the portraits of her parents-in-law, Joel and Esther Farr Knight, accompany this recollection in the history of Dummerston, Vt. In all, there are three pairs of Belknap portraits of Knight family members; portraits of Asa's brother, Joel, and sister-in-law, Fanny Duncan Knight, are also owned by a descendant.[1]

This youthful image of his mother, with her fashionable turban and pleated round collar, must have stayed with Randolph throughout his life. Recalling her "beauty and cheerful demeanor," he described her as "a great reader [who] long took a lively interest in all the events concerning the welfare of our country, the proceedings of Congress and news from abroad. The extensive acquaintance of her husband brought within her doors a large number of prominent people in the country and state who remember...her sweet face, pleasant ways and generous hospitality."[2]

In the early 1830s, when the portraits were painted, Asa Knight had been for about six years, the proprietor of a small, well-stocked, general store. The daybook and ledger behind him are symbols of his business. Filled with daily accounts and postings to each of his customers, these books reveal how he sold the goods that he purchased on biannual trips to Boston. His customers received store credit for such country produce as poultry, butter and cheese, and later in the 1830s, palm leaf hats.

Asa Knight's personal history was a Dummerston success story. His grandfather had been one of the town's earliest settlers in 1774. His father, Joel, enlisted in the Continental Army in 1780, saw action, and was granted a pension in 1833. Joel married Esther Farr in 1786, and Asa, born in 1793, grew up a farmer's son. At the age of 21 he was commissioned an orderly sergeant in the Vermont militia,[3] and he took his place on the list of town officers in 1819, when he was elected constable and tax collector for the first of four one-year terms. About the same time, he also accepted appointment as deputy sheriff of Windham County. He and Susan Miller, who was also from an old Dummerston family, were married in the spring of 1822 and shortly afterwards moved to nearby Newfane, where Knight became the keeper of the county jail.

Late in 1826 Knight purchased Adin Thayer's store at the south end of the Dummerston common and prepared it for opening the following April. In that month the deed was recorded and Knight was ready for business with a stock of spring goods and the prospect of trading butter and cheese from Dummerston dairies in Boston at the Faneuil Market stall of Daniel Taylor, his cousin by marriage.[4]

In addition to keeping store, Knight played a prominent role in town, county and state government, especially during the 1830s, when the portraits were painted. He was a Dummerston selectman for seven years, justice of the peace from 1831 to 1848, Windham County's Judge of Probate for two years, and a representative in the Vermont legislature for four years. Prospering, in the mid-1830s Knight built a two-and-a-half story addition to the store, with the gable end facing the town common.[5]

By the time Knight re-opened this larger store in 1838, Dummerston's population was seriously contracting and the nation was in the throes of the Panic of 1837. Knight withdrew from public service and reorganized his business. He entered into one partnership between 1838 and 1842 and another between 1846 and 1848. Knight and his business were rated eight times between 1842 and 1851; the business was deemed thriving or safe each time, but claims against his estate after his death in July 1851 exceeded the value of his real and personal property by $1616.27.[6]

Susan Knight, assisted by several of Knight's friends, settled her husband's estate. She received the family homestead, where she raised the three youngest of her seven children, and lived there until her death in 1884. With the exception of one daughter, who lived at home and never married, her children, like so many of Dummerston's younger sons and daughters, dispersed—to neighboring Brattleboro, Boston, Iowa, California, and Maryland.

[CS]

Top: Cat. 51; below: Cat. 52

[1] David L. Mansfield, *The History of the Town of Dummerston*, (Ludlow, Vt: A.M. Hemenway, 1884), 144, 120, 143.

[2] Mansfield, *History of Dummerston*, 144-5.

[3] Commission, Old Sturbridge Village Research Library.

[4] The operations of the Knight Store are described in detail in Caroline Fuller Sloat, "The Center of Local Commerce: The Asa Knight Store of Dummerston, Vt., 1827-1851," *Vermont History*, 53 (Fall 1985): 205-220.

[5] The Knight store was moved to Old Sturbridge Village and opened to the public in 1973, adding commerce and trade to the Museum's interpretation of everyday life in rural New England.

[6] Windham County, Vt., Probate Records, Courthouse, Newfane, 20: 343-5.

53.
NANCY LAWSON (1803-?)
William Matthew Prior (1806-1873)
Boston, Mass., 1843
30 x 25 (76.2 x 63.5)
Inscribed lower right: *Nancy Lawson, May 11 1843./ W. M. Prior*
Shelburne Museum, Shelburne, Vt.
Plate 2

54.
WILLIAM LAWSON (1800-?)
William Matthew Prior (1806-1873)
Boston, Mass., 1843
Oil on canvas
30 x 25 (76.2 x 63.5)
Inscribed lower right: *W. Lawson, May 2nd 1843/ By W. M. Prior*
Shelburne Museum, Shelburne, Vt.
Plate 3

WILLIAM AND NANCY LAWSON'S arresting likenesses are rarities. Few New Englanders of African descent—one percent of the region's population—sat for portraits. Earlier collectors of American art identified Lawson conjecturally as an abolitionist and incorrectly as a minister. In fact, he was listed as a clothing merchant in the "People of Color" listings of the Boston city directories between 1841 and 1850. The 1850 census further identified the couple as natives of Massachusetts, with a daughter living at home.[1] Both Lawsons are well dressed and confidently posed in these paintings. William is shown with a resplendent watch fob and a smoldering cigar, while Nancy's clothes are colorful and fashionable. They were members of New England's small and precariously poised African-American middle class, and their attire and accoutrements, which are fully in keeping with Lawson's trade, suggest pride in their material achievements.

William Lawson cannot be linked specifically to the abolition movement, but Prior's portraiture does suggest linkages with both antislavery and anti-racist feeling. Prior's documented work includes a number of paintings of African-Americans, substantially more than that of any other New England artist. With his Boston studio, which operated for three decades beginning in 1841, Prior was accessible to the members of New England's largest African-American community, and there is evidence that he sought out their patronage. Given the pervasive racism of American society, North and South, a white painter's portrayal of black people with confident posture and affluent dress was a bold undertaking. It is striking that Prior (cats. 42, 43, 57, 80), who did not usually sign his paintings, inscribed his name on the front of both Lawson portraits. Equally unusual is the identification of each sitter on the face of the portraits, affirming their importance as individuals. Several students of Prior's work have suggested that his sympathy for African-Americans stemmed from his devout participation in the Adventist Movement, started by the preacher William Miller, whose followers were staunch supporters of the abolitionist cause.[2]

[JL]

[1] Population Schedules, Boston, Mass., U.S. Census, 1850, 335: 208 (microfilm).

[2] D'Ambrosio and Emans, *Folk Art's Many Faces*, 133-141.

Right: Cats. 53 and 54; photographs by Ken Burris

55.
MARY LOCKE
Ruth Henshaw Bascom (1772-1848)
Lowell, Mass., 1829
Pastel, pencil, and gold foil on paper
17 1/4 x 12 1/2 (43.8 x 31 75)
Inscribed verso: *Miss Mary Locke, Lowell / Taken Oct 1829*
Private Collection

UNMISTAKABLY FROM the hand of Ruth Bascom (cat. 11), this profile shows the artist's transition to techniques that characterize her more mature work. Her earlier likenesses were set against solid backgrounds, usually blue or white, but in the late 1820s she began experimenting with more decorative backdrops such as the shaded oval seen in this portrait. Many of her works from the following decade feature subjects framed with drapery or flanked by trees (see cat. 23). Less frequently, Bascom applied bits of metallic foil to a profile to highlight jewelry, buttons, hair ornaments, eyeglasses, or earrings. The four small beads of Mary Locke's necklace are made of gold foil.

Cat. 55

At the time of the portrait sitting, Bascom was living in Ashby, Mass., about thirty miles from Lowell, but her journal for 1829 does not record traveling to Lowell or taking Mary Locke's likeness. There are, however, frequent references to Esquire John G. Locke of Ashby and his brother, Albert. It is very likely that they were relatives of Mary Locke, as nearly all of Bascom's portraits are of people to whom she was connected through family or friends.

56.
EDWARD MELLEN (1802-?)
Artist Unknown
Wayland or Worcester, Mass., c. 1840-1850
Watercolor on ivory
9 1/2 x 6 1/2 (24.2 x 16.5)
Old Sturbridge Village

THE MODEST SCALE of this portrait seems to contradict its intent to honor Edward Mellen's accomplishments. The three-quarter-length likeness of Mellen, shown with his library, is in the tradition of portraits exalting men in the "learned professions." Such images were usually on a scale consistent with their grand purpose. The size of this painting probably reflects Mellen's personal preference. There certainly would have been no economic advantage to choosing a watercolor miniature instead of an oil portrait, for the two media were roughly equivalent in price, and this detailed miniature might even have cost slightly more.

Further contradictions make the precise date of this image difficult to establish. Mellen's clothing reflects the styles of the 1830s, but the furnishings around him suggest the late 1840s, as does his evident middle age. It may have been painted in 1847, when the Middlesex County lawyer became an associate justice for the Court of Common Pleas in Worcester, Mass.[1] The books with which Mellen is portrayed allude to his education at Brown University and to his profession. The classical column to his left suggests the roots of the judicial system and of institutional architecture.

While Mellen was on the Worcester bench, he boarded in that city, maintaining a permanent residence in Wayland, where his wife and six children resided.[2] In 1854 he became chief justice, a position he held until 1859.[3] In that year the Court of Common Pleas was abolished and replaced by the Superior

Court. Mellen then returned to his law practice at the age of fifty-seven and found "his long inexperience in the advocacy of causes had left his weapons rusty, and dulled the force of his attacks."[4] He established his practice in Worcester, perhaps to build on connections made during his judicial career. He maintained an office in Worcester through the 1860s, first in partnership with W.S. Davis, and later alone.[5]

[1] *History of Worcester County, Mass. with Biographical Sketches*, comp. D. Hamilton Hurd, I (Philadelphia: J.W. Lewis & Co., 1889), xiiii.
[2] *V.R.*, Wayland, Mass., 30.
[3] Caleb A. Wall, *Reminiscences of Worcester* (Worcester: Tyler and Seagrave, 1877), 219.
[4] Hurd, *History of Worcester*, xiiii.
[5] Howland, *The Worcester Almanac, Directory, and Business Advertiser for 1862*, 106; *...for 1864*, 80; *The Worcester Directory for 1865*, 86; *...for 1868*, 172.

Cat. 56

57.
TWO CHILDREN OF THE MORSE FAMILY AND THEIR DOG MINNY
William Matthew Prior (1806-1873)
Boston, Mass., c. 1841-45
Oil on canvas
28 x 32 (71.1 x 81.3)
Inscribed on dog's collar: *Minny Morse*
Old Sturbridge Village

WILLIAM MATTHEW PRIOR established a studio in Boston in 1841 and lived and worked in that city for most of the following thirty-one years. During the second half of that period his business as a portrait painter declined, possibly due to competition from a growing number of photographic portrait studios. The years between 1841 and 1855, however, were a prolific period for the artist. His vivid and affordable portraits secured him a place as the painter of the urban middle class, and he was patronized by prosperous merchants, artisans and other tradesmen.

Of the known Prior portraits from this period, there are roughly twice as many of children as of adults. This survival rate may be purely a reflection of modern collecting interests, for images of children have a special charm. Nonetheless, the fact that Prior painted so many children suggests that he established a reputation for himself in that genre. As do his other portraits (see. cats. 42, 43, 53, 54, 80), Prior's paintings of children cover the spectrum from hasty two-dimensionality to fairly academic work. All of these works are linked by Prior's distinctive style and by shared compositional devices and props.

This portrait of two children represents a middle ground in Prior's work. It is not one of his cheapest, flat likenesses, but it does demonstrate the use of a formula to speed his work. In depicting the children, Prior defines their forms mostly in flat blocks of color, as in the older girl's black hair and blue dress. This is a common device in his individual and group portraits of children, as is the composition built around seated figures. Black and white dogs, lace-edged pantalettes, and toys are also common sights in Prior's likenesses of children. Yet, despite this formulaic quality there are enough individualizing details to personalize the painting. The dog is "Minny Morse," not a generic pet. Neither is the baby an icon of childhood, but a

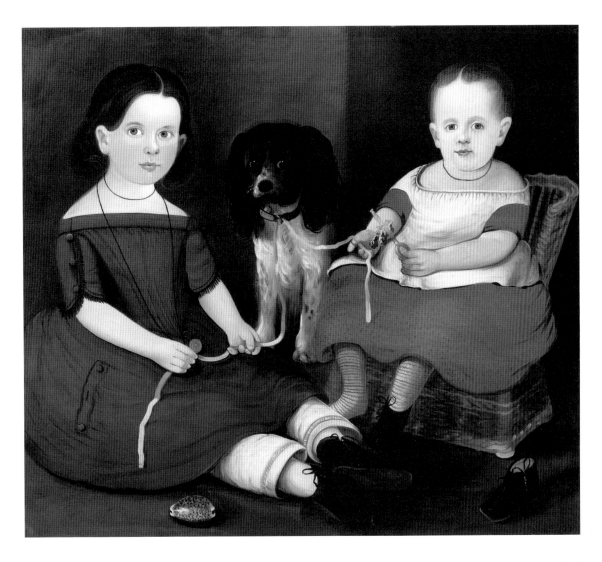

restless toddler who has kicked off a shoe and requires coral and bells to provide distraction and soothe gums sore from teething.

58.
JOEL NEGUS (1768-1816)
Nathan Negus (1801-1825)
Probably Georgia, c. 1821
Oil on canvas
Inscribed verso: *Joel Negus. Painted five years after his death by his son, Nathan Negus.*
28 x 24 (71.1 x 61)
Petersham Historical Society, Inc., Petersham, Mass.

BY ALL ACCOUNTS JOEL NEGUS was a man of many talents and a pleasing manner, much loved by his large family.[1] He lived in a one-story gambrel-roofed house on the common in Petersham, Mass., with his wife, Basmeth Gould, and the twelve of their fourteen children who survived infancy.[2] To support this large family he pieced together a livelihood by farming ten acres and working alternately as a teacher, a house and sign painter, a surveyor, and a woodworker.[3] He prospered through his enterprises, acquiring additional farm and wood lands, so that when he died in 1816 he left an estate valued at $3451.67.[4]

Negus's untimely death was precipitated by being thrown from a sleigh down an embankment. He survived this accident for a year or two, but never regained his health.[5] During his invalidism, his children's correspondence shows their grief as his vitality declined and their gradual reconciliation to the inevitability of his death. The summer before he died,

most sincerely do I return you my thanks for the emotion you took in painting Joseph portrait. I am very well satisfied with it, it is known by every one that sees it. It is a pleasure & pain for me to look at it.[8]

Joel Negus's portrait was painted in Georgia, where Nathan was living in 1821. The painting apparently was given to the widowed Elizabeth Negus, for in 1824 she wrote to the family in Massachusetts that she had a pair of portraits of Joel and Basmeth.[9] A year later she promised: "I will send your fathers portrait with pleasure for I think you have the best right to it although I sett by it. I shall not be able to send it until winter."[10] By then Nathan, too, had died, and for the Neguses the portrait became a memorial to both father and son.

Negus traveled to Saratoga Springs in the hope of restoring his health.[6] That trip failed to effect any change, and Negus died in November 1816.

Negus had been the emotional and economic center of his family. Following the accident his household lost its cohesion as the eight eldest children left home to find work or to reside with relatives. Within seven years of Negus's death his widow gave up housekeeping and she and her two youngest daughters became dependent on other family members (see cats. 33, 59, 73, 74).

This posthumous portrait calls to mind the sentiment of another New Englander in commissioning a portrait of her mother: "Don't you think it will be very pleasant to [have] her portrait to look at when she is in the grave?"[7] That idea may have guided Nathan Negus (cat. 59) when he painted his father's likeness from memory. Called upon to create other images of family members after they died, Nathan painted a posthumous portrait of his brother Joseph for his widowed sister-in-law, Elizabeth. She wrote appreciatively from Alabama:

[1] Benjamin Howe, "Sketch of the Negus and Fuller Families", unpublished manuscript, Pocumtuck Valley Memorial Association Library, Deerfield, Mass.; J.B. Howe, *Sketches of Petersham Natives and Adopted Citizens* (1915).
[2] V.R., Petersham, Mass.; Mabel Coolidge Cook, *The History of Petersham, Mass.* (The Petersham Historical Society, n.d.), 58-59, 149.
[3] Worcester County Probate Records, docket #42748, Joel Negus Inventory; Correspondence, Joel Negus to Arathusa Negus, 1809-1810, Petersham Historical Society (PHS), Petersham, Mass.
[4] Records of Estate Administration.
[5] Howe, "Sketch of the Negus and Fuller Families", 5-6.
[6] Fuller/Negus Papers.
[7] Sarah Clapp to John Clapp, 7 May 1844, Clapp Family Papers, American Antiquarian Society, Worcester, Mass.
[8] Elizabeth Filcont Negus to Nathan Negus, 24 September 1824, PHS.
[9] Elizabeth Filcont Negus to Fanny Negus Fuller, 10 October 1824, PHS.
[10] Elizabeth Filcont Negus to Laura Negus, 25 August 1825, PHS.

59.
SELF-PORTRAIT OF NATHAN NEGUS
(1801-1825)
Massachusetts, c. 1820
Oil on canvas
22 1/8 X 18 1/4
Pocumtuck Valley Memorial Association,
Memorial Hall Museum, Deerfield, Mass.

THIS IS ONE OF FOUR KNOWN self-portraits by Nathan Negus. Found beneath a later self-portrait, this canvas has been substantially overpainted (by a descendant) on the torso and background, but the rendering of the face is in the artist's hand. Negus's memorandum book for 1819-1821 notes work on self-images such as "fixed up a room...and began to paint my portrait."[1] This and other entries reveal that the artist developed his skill at taking likenesses by practicing on himself and family members.

Nathan Negus's letters and memorandum book provide unusually complete documentation of the education and experiences of an itinerant artist. He offers an especially concise case study because his life was so short, yet comprehended a full ten years of focused artistic activity, first as an apprentice and then as a traveling portrait, sign, and ornamental painter.

Born in Petersham, Mass., on 20 March 1801, Nathan was the seventh of Basmeth and Joel Negus's (cat. 58) fourteen children.[2] Said to have shown native artistic ability, he was encouraged to follow his father, a house and sign painter, in cultivating his talents into a source of livelihood.[3] His training was in all the "branches of painting"[4], accommodating his ambition to be an artist while developing the more marketable skills of a fancy painter.

At the age of thirteen, Negus went to Boston to study with the portraitist Ethan Allen Greenwood. He wrote to his brother that he planned to spend a month or two in Greenwood's studio "for the purpose of getting some knowledge of limnering."[5] Later that year, he entered an apprenticeship in the Boston shop of the ornamental painter John Ritto Penniman, who instructed many other artists, including Alvan Fisher and Jane Stuart.[6] During the five years he spent under Penniman's tutelage, Negus lettered store drawers, ornamented fire buckets and organ boards, made drawings for patent applications, painted signs and standards, and decorated Masonic aprons (fig.19).

While living in Boston, Negus augmented his artistic education by attending lectures and the theater, visiting galleries to view pictures, and accepting portrait commissions. He and several friends formed a "society for the instruction of young artists," which they archly named the Pennimanic Society.[7] This group of nine met monthly to hear discourses on art, and they visited art centers like the Gallery of Fine Arts, the New England Museum, and the Artists' Association Hall.

Despite these activities, Negus chafed within the constraints of apprenticeship and was eager to be free to pursue his career. Entries in his journal are tinged with resentment of his duties, as when he wrote "by

Mr. P.'s request I went to work in the cold damp shop...caught a bad cold."[8] The admonishment from Negus's family to be "dutifull and obediant, to all [Mr. Penniman's] commands (if reasonable)" suggests that they knew there was friction between apprentice and master.[9] An episode illustrative of the subordinate nature of apprenticeship, which may have contributed to this tension, took place in the fall of 1819. Negus spent a week at the end of October painting a fifteen-foot view of the burning of the Exchange Coffee House, probably after a cartoon drawn by Penniman.

On 3 November, the anniversary of the fire, the painting was exhibited in the Gallery of Fine Arts, where it met with "great applause" but was credited to the hand of Penniman.[10] While appreciation of the painting must have gratified the young artist, he surely rankled when his master received the public praise.

An apprenticeship was a contractual agreement that bound a young man to his master's shop until the age of twenty-one. Halfway through Negus's indenture he learned that Penniman had mistaken his birth

Cat. 59

date. As he explained to his sister in 1818, "Mr. Penniman thinks I am eighteen, and I should wish to have you make folks think so up there, for this is a comfortable thing for me to be free at the age of

Fig. 19 Masonic Apron, Nathan Negus, Boston, Mass., 1817, opaque watercolor on satin-woven silk, 17 3/4 x 16 3/4 (45.6 x 42.5), Museum of Our National Heritage, Lexington, Mass.

twenty."[11] The ruse proved unnecessary, for in May 1820 illness liberated Negus from Penniman's shop and helped launch his career as an itinerant artist. He left Boston for Petersham, stopping in Fitchburg to visit friends and recuperate. There he found ample patronage and stayed eight weeks during which he drew nine miniatures and painted seven portraits. He secured these commissions by visiting prominent members of the community, dining with them, and initially promoting his talents by giving gifts of India ink likenesses. On average his portraits earned six dollars, although once he was paid with six volumes of Shakespeare's plays. When he left Fitchburg, Negus "received a recommendation from Esq. Willard, signed by all the gentlemen of note in that town."[12]

After spending the summer of 1820 traveling around northern New England, Negus began to prepare for a

trip to the South. In 1819, his brother Joseph, a merchant in Georgia, had proposed a partnership, combining his business acumen with Nathan's artistic abilities. He estimated that they "would make money very fast in the southern states for a year or two at portrait painting together with painting some rooms for wealthy men who would pay an extravagant price."[13] In September 1820, Joseph sent Nathan one hundred and forty dollars, asking him to "save enough to pay your expenses and lay the rest out in paints &c." He went on to detail the materials they would need:

> We shall want a quintity of Ivory to paint miniatures an a good asortment of tools of every disscription, both for Portrait, ornimental & room painting, with a paint stone &c. 2 or 3 Doz. Books gold leaf & paints suitable for Portraits & miniatures. The other paints that we shall want we can get about as well in Savannah as Boston.[14]

In November Negus went to Boston to "collect…articles for painting," before setting sail for Savannah on the Brig Eagle out of Providence.[15] On arriving in Georgia, he rented space for "Negus' Painting Room" for fifteen dollars a month. He was soon busy painting oil portraits, miniatures, Masonic aprons, a floorcloth, and pieces for embroidery.[16]

In March 1821 the Negus brothers set off on a one-year journey. Using Eatonton, Ga., as a base, they painted signs, Masonic halls, standards, and portraits. Nathan found ongoing work painting scenery for the Thespians, a theater group in Eatonton, and had a fairly steady flow of commissions. In April 1821 the brothers began to paint the Masonic Hall at Milledgeville, Ga.—"the wall in Distemper, the wood work in oil for 150 Dollars."[17] At the end of July that year, they went to the Creek Indians's lands, where Nathan painted a "portrait in full length" of William MacIntosh, the Creek leader.[18]

Although Joseph had rudimentary artistic abilities and assisted with decorative painting jobs, Nathan did most of the work. Unfortunately, Joseph spent money faster than Nathan could earn it and the partners were habitually in debt. Their debts grew when family members made loans to them. By July 1822 Joseph had married Elizabeth Filcont of Massachusetts and began planning to establish a carriage factory in Alabama.[19] Shortly after the marriage, the brothers' partnership was dissolved and Nathan, having cleared his personal and business debts, moved to Mobile to "commence...life entirely anew."[20]

Negus went to the south to exploit its business opportunities, but once there he found it a hospitable climate for his frail health. In 1822, he wrote to his sister that he hoped to come home but was waiting until "the rigors of winter passes by at the North."[21] While he enjoyed the mild southern winters, he found the intense heat of summer debilitating, and hoped to spend "winters at the South and summers at the North."[22]

The last two years of Negus's life were plagued by illness. Those who knew him recalled "he never experienced a day of real health."[23] He was diagnosed with "slow consumption," a progressive wasting of the body associated with pulmonary tuberculosis.[24] His disease caused chronic chest pain and a bad cough. He also suffered colds, fevers, attacks of typhus, and "the liver complaint." His condition was not improved by his medical treatment, which included bleeding and doses of mercury, nitric acid, and other purgatives.

On arriving in Mobile, Ala., he found that his "popularity as an eminent artist" brought him lucrative employment.[25] At the end of the winter in 1823, Negus returned to Massachusetts to visit his family and to make arrangements for a more settled future. He hoped to make the transition from itinerancy to working in a studio or his home. A central element in this plan was marriage, but the object of his affections, upon seeing the ruinous state of his health, declined his proposal.[26]

Having failed to realize his "vision of connubial felicity" Negus resolved to establish an academy where he would teach drawing and painting.[27] To that end he went to study perspective with a Mr. Jackson in Milton, Mass. His expenses were to be paid by a friend who was in debt to him, but when the friend did not pay, Negus became liable for expenses he could not meet. Pursued by bailiffs, he boarded a ship for Alabama. He was impoverished, disappointed by love and friendship, and in disgrace with his family, whom he had failed to visit and who feared he would not live to see them again. In the midst of this drama, Negus received word of the death of his brother and arrived in Alabama to face the dismal task of administering Joseph's deeply indebted estate.[28]

It had always been Negus's intention to return to the South for one more season to fulfill a contract to paint scenery for the New Theater in Mobile. When he made his escape from Boston late in 1823, this job as a scene painter beckoned as a secure situation that paid fifty dollars a week.[29] Negus remained in Mobile for a year and a half, working for the New Theater and battling increasingly frequent and debilitating bouts of illness. By the end of May 1825 his physical condition was sufficiently dire that he decided to return to Massachusetts. According to family history, his ship was becalmed for twenty-eight days in the Gulf of Mexico and he did not arrive in Boston until mid-July. Friends helped the critically ill artist travel home to Petersham, where he died on 19 July 1825, four days after his return.[30]

Fig. 20 John Robinson, Nathan Negus, Oakham, Mass.,
c. 1820, ink and watercolor on paper, 6 1/8 x 5 1/8 (15.5 x 13),
Petersham Historical Society, Inc.

As an unmarried man without a permanent residence, Negus left an understandably modest estate. Valued at $111.88, his personal property consisted almost entirely of clothing and painting supplies. Unfortunately, his art materials were not enumerated but grouped as a paint box and stone valued at $2.25, forty brushes and paints worth $6.70, and paintings appraised at $5.25. His clothing is listed in much greater detail and reveals a fastidious young man concerned about his appearance—an impression also conveyed by his self-portraits. Negus's wardrobe, valued at $69, included thirteen shirts, three pairs of pantaloons, five vests, two tailcoats, a cravat, and other accessories. His large supply of shirts—roughly three times the average—would have permitted him to wear clean linen whenever he appeared in public, one of the central tenets of genteel behavior. His ownership of a toothbrush, a somewhat uncommon object in 1825, shows his awareness of personal hygiene.[31] His illness may have heightened his concern for cleanliness, but his work may also account for it. Traveling to communities where he was unknown, his appearance and deportment would have been critical in encouraging patronage.

The Negus family actively sought to document and preserve Nathan's history with manuscripts and paintings, yielding an extraordinary record. After a visit to Boston in 1826, Fanny Negus Fuller wrote to her brother-in-law "I got Nathan's Portrait that he said so much about." She went on to describe an exchange in which "Greenwood was unwilling to give [the portrait] up saying Nathan made a present of [it] to him but I cried like a calf...[and] he came to his feelings & gave it to me."[32]

It is unfortunate that more portraits by Nathan Negus have not been identified, but those that are known show him to have been a gifted and skillful artist. His journal and letters provide a revealing look at art as an early 19th-century craft that was viewed as a viable profession. For young men like him, work as an itinerant painter offered, as one commentator observed, "the means of introducing a young man to the best society and...the means of establishing himself advantageously in the world."[33] For artists of talent and initiative, work as a traveling artisan-painter often led to additional academic training and the establishment of a studio in an urban center. This was a progression successfully navigated by artists such as

Charles Bird King (cats. 75, 76, plate 11) and Francis Alexander (cat. 22), but one that Negus did not live long enough to realize.

[1] Nathan Negus, 17 July 1820, Memorandum Book for 1819, 1820, and 1821, Fuller/Negus Papers. Except where noted, all correspondence cited is from this collection.
[2] *V.R.*, Petersham, Mass..
[3] Howe, *Sketches of Petersham*, 40-41.
[4] Joseph Negus to Nathan Negus, 26 March 1820.
[5] Nathan Negus to Joseph Negus, 28 February 1815.
[6] Carol Damon Andrews, "John Ritto Penniman (1782-1841), an ingenious New England artist," *Antiques*, 120 (July 1981): 147-170.
[7] 21 October 1819, Memorandum Book.
[8] 11 September 1819, Memorandum Book.
[9] Rosanna Negus to Nathan Negus, 3 January 1817, Petersham Historical Society (PHS).
[10] 27 October-3 November 1819, Memorandum Book; *The Columbian Centinel*, 3 November 1819.
[11] Nathan Negus to Laura Negus, 26 February 1818, PHS.
[12] 29 June 1820, see also 4 May-28 June 1820, Memorandum Book.
[13] Joseph Negus to Nathan Negus, 28 December 1819, quoted in Agnes M. Dods, "Nathan and Joseph Negus, Itinerant Painters," *Antiques*, 76 (November 1959): 436.
[14] Joseph Negus to Nathan Negus, 10 September 1820.
[15] 6 November, 20 November 1820, Memorandum Book.
[16] 8 December 1820-6 March 1821, Memorandum Book.
[17] 2 April 1821, Memorandum Book; while in Milledgeville, Joseph and Nathan had the first three degrees of Freemasonry conferred upon them and were accepted into the lodge.
[18] Week of 23 July 1821, Memorandum Book; MacIntosh's portrait is illustrated in Dods, "Nathan and Joseph Negus," 435.
[19] Nathan Negus to Fanny Fuller, July 1822, quoted in Dods, "Nathan and Joseph Negus," 436.
[20] Nathan Negus to Jonas Howe, 14 January c. 1824.
[21] Nathan Negus to Laura Negus, 25 July 1822.
[21] Nathan Negus to his family, 27 July 1824.
[22] Howe, *Petersham Sketches*, 41.
[23] Nathan Negus to his family, 27 July 1824.
[24] Nathan Negus to Jonas Howe, 14 January c. 1824.
[25] Nathan Negus to his family, 27 July 1824.
[26] Nathan Negus to Aaron Fuller, October 1824.
[26] Nathan Negus to his family, 27 July 1824.
[27] Nathan Negus to unknown, c. 1824-25.
[28] Conclusion to Nathan Negus's correspondence written by Elizabeth Fuller.
[29] Worcester County, Probate Records, docket #42757, Nathan Negus, Inventory, 61: 586; "Bill of Articles from Estate of N.N."
[30] Fanny Fuller to Jonas Howe, 13 August 1826, PHS.
[31] John Vanderlyn to John Vanderlyn Jr., 9 September 1825, quoted in David Jaffee, "One of the Primitive Sort: Portrait Makers of the Rural North 1760-1860", in *The Countryside in the Age of Capitalist Transformation*, eds. Steven Hahn and Jonathan Prude (Chapel Hill, NC: The University of North Carolina Press, 1985), 103.

60.
POSSIBLY A MEMBER
OF THE PAYLY FAMILY
Ruth Henshaw Bascom (1772-1848)
Probably southern New Hampshire, c. 1840
Pastel on paper
18 1/2 x 14 1/2 (47 x 36.9)
Old Sturbridge Village

ALTHOUGH THIS PORTRAIT is reputed to be of a young member of the Payly family of Fitzwilliam, N.H., early-19th-century population censuses for that town do not list any Paylys. The association with Fitzwilliam may stem from the fact that Bascom lived there from 1839 to 1841, the years during which this work appears to have been executed. The child's hairstyle and dress bodice are in the fashions of that period. Stylistically this work exemplifies Bascom's later technique, when she often set her subjects against abstract landscapes. The artist seems to have enjoyed portraying young people, for roughly a third of her known likenesses are of children.[1]

Cat.60

[1] Lois S. Avigad, "Ruth Henshaw Bascom, A Youthful Viewpoint", *The Clarion*, 12 (Fall 1987): 35- 41.

61.
JOHN PERRIN (1803-1893)
Royall Brewster Smith (1801-1855)
Maine, 1835
Oil on canvas
31 1/8 x 26 1/8 (79.1 x 66.4)
Old Sturbridge Village

THE BLACK CRAVAT AND TAILCOAT worn by the Reverend John Perrin typify male formal attire in the 1830s, a style adopted by most New England clergymen of the time. Only a few decades earlier clergymen had donned robes for preaching, such as the one depicted in the portrait of Reverend Nathanial Howe (cat. 44). This secularization of dress reflects a rise in religious diversity and the decline in the dominance of the Congregational Church. Although religion remained a primary force in New England in the 19th century, a greater variety of religious choices was then available. One option was the Methodist church, in which John Perrin was a minister.

In his portrait, Perrin is portrayed in the act of

Cat. 61

writing; resting beneath his hand is a sheet of paper that bears the words, "John Perrin: Four volumes of religious works. Dec. 1835." This inscription is puzzling, as no published works by John Perrin have been found; however, the portrait emphasizes the role of the minister as an interpreter. Through writing and preaching, a minister was able to bring ideas to many people. This is further expressed in Perrin's portrait with the proclamation, "with no other weapon than the gospel the Missionaries of the cross have caused the habitations of savage cruelty to be clothed in the weakness of the lamb." As an itinerant minister, Perrin was a missionary, whose objective was to introduce Methodist beliefs to New England's rural, and predominantly Congregational, communities.

As a clergyman, Perrin (a Vermont native) traveled in Maine and New Hampshire. He moved often, never remaining in one town for more than two years. From 1829 through 1838 he worked in southern Maine. The minutes of the Methodist conference there describe him as "retired" between 1836-38.[1] His frequent travels, which make it difficult to document the details of his life, nevertheless continued, although he does not reappear in church records until 1858, when he was in New Hampshire. He continued his ministry until 1863.

Perrin's itinerant life in Maine and New Hampshire paralleled Royall Brewster Smith's career as a traveling artist. Born in Buxton, Smith worked chiefly in southern Maine in towns such as Gorham, Limington, Newfield, Saco, Sebago, and Standish. All of his known work was done in the 1830s, and while few of his paintings are signed, his distinctive style and compositional devices identify them. Perrin's portrait is nearly identical to a likeness of Joseph Brown, which features its subject writing biographical information with a quill pen. In 1835, Perrin was in Newfield, Me., a town that Smith is known to have visited, and the minister and the artist may have met there.[2]

[1] *Minutes of the Annual Conferences of the Methodist Episcopal Church for the Years 1829-1839*, II (New York, 1840), 328, 461.
[2] Arthur and Sybil Kern, "Painted by Royall B. Smith," *The Clarion* 13 (Spring 1988): 48-55.

Top: Cat. 62; below: Cat. 63

62.
HANNAH CHANDLER PERRY
(1808-1899)
Aaron Dean Fletcher (1817-1902)
Saxtons River, Vt., c. 1837
Oil on canvas
28 1/4 x 24 (71.8 x 61)
Old Sturbridge Village

63.
GEORGE PERRY (1807-1854)
Aaron Dean Fletcher (1817-1902)
Saxtons River, Vt., c. 1837
Oil on canvas
28 1/4 x 24 (71.8 x 61)
Old Sturbridge Village

64.
SOLON PERRY (1829-1905)
Aaron Dean Fletcher (1817-1902)
Saxtons River, Vt., c. 1837
Oil on canvas
25 3/4 x 23 1/4 (65.4 x 59.1)
Private Collection

65.
MARY PERRY (1839-?)
Unknown Artist
Saxtons River, Vt., c. 1844
Oil on canvas
31 1/2 x 24 1/2 (80 x 62.2)
Private Collection

GEORGE PERRY, A PROSPERING tin manufacturer, commissioned portraits of his family from a local artist, Aaron Dean Fletcher, as did the Adams family (cats. 2-5), who lived in the neighboring countryside. His choice may have been influenced by kinship, for Fletcher was his mother's fifth cousin; and like most rural portrait painters, Fletcher traveled among a network of family and friends to secure work.[1] When the Perrys were painted, they had only one child, Solon. Mary was born two years later, and the family group was not completed until the mid-1840s, when another artist was employed to take her likeness, Fletcher having moved to New York state by then.

Leaning back from his desk and gazing assuredly

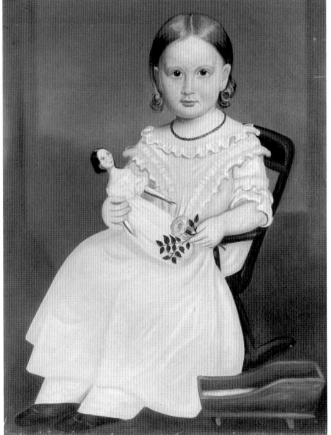

Top: Cat. 64; below: Cat. 65; photographs by Chuck Kidd

out from his portrait, George Perry has the air of a prospering businessman. In 1831, he had left his work as a farmer to start a tinware manufacturing business with his brother Fletcher.[2] Their shop was located in the village of Saxtons River and sold tin articles that they made, as well as "trunk goods" such as combs, sewing notions, knives, and roach traps. A network of peddlers distributed their stock throughout northern New England and into New York.[3]

The Perrys's flourishing business withstood the financial panic of 1837. Although "the panic struck the manufacturing interests of the little village," a local history recounts that "the Perrys went right on making money."[4] In the 1840s, they sold their shop and shifted their investments to the lucrative production of woolens. George Perry & Co., textile manufacturers, opened in 1847 and operated for twenty years, with Solon Perry managing the business after his father's death in 1858.[5] The estate was valued at $58,975.87, clear evidence of George Perry's success.[6]

These portraits reflect the comfort and prosperity of the Perry home. Hannah is garbed quietly but elegantly. Colorful accents are provided by a handsome green shawl and a gold ring, brooch, and earrings. Only the small thimble worn on her cupped right hand alludes to her domestic labors. Solon, like Hiram Adams (cat. 5), is dressed in a modish frock coat and posed with his pet dog. When this picture was painted, young Perry was not yet a classmate of Adams's at the Saxtons River Academy, where both boys were enrolled by 1844.[7] The academy was founded in 1842 with the financial support of townspeople including George and Fletcher Perry.

About the time Solon matriculated to the academy his younger sister had her portrait painted. It offers a more detailed environment than the Fletcher portraits, showing a pampered little girl. Mary is shown sitting in a child-size rocking chair and cuddling a French *papier maché* doll with a toy cradle at her feet. Although the rose she holds and her necklace are fairly standard elements in little girls' portraits, the specialized furniture and toys in this painting were available only to affluent New England families.

[1] Burdick and Muller, "Aaron Dean Fletcher," 184-193.
[2] Hamilton Child, *Gazetteer and Business Directory of Windham County, Vt., 1724-1884* (Syracuse, NY, 1884), 304.
[3] Shirley Spaulding DeVoe, "The Perry Tin Shop of Saxtons River, Vt.," *Vermont History*, 43 (1975): 204-207.
[4] *Bellows Falls Times*, 8 April 1899.
[5] Hayes, *History of Rockingham*, 726.
[6] Rockingham County, Vt., Probate Records, Bellows Falls, Account of the Administrators of the Estate of George Perry, 22: 322.
[7] *Catalogue of Officers, Instructors and Students of Saxtons River Academy, Rockingham, Vt.* (Bellows Falls, 1844), cited in Burdick and Muller, "Aaron Dean Fletcher," 184.

Cat. 66

66.
THREE CHILDREN OF THE PRATT FAMILY
Jones Fawson Morris (1801- c. 1838)
Sterling, Mass., c. 1834-1838
Oil on canvas
26 x 22 (66 x 55.8)
Inscribed verso: *Jones F. Morris*
Private Collection

MANY NON-ACADEMIC ARTISTS, such as Nathan Negus (cat. 59) and Nathaniel Hamblen (cat. 80), were the second or third generation of painters in their families. This is true of Jones Fawson Morris, the son of a decorative painter who immigrated to Sterling, Mass., from England.[1] During the 1830s, Jones Morris painted portraits for many local families, among them the Bartletts (cats. 9, 10).

The Pratt family also patronized the artist, as this painting and a surviving portrait of Lieutenant Joel Pratt attest.[2] Until its recent sale at auction, this painting of three children remained in one of the Pratt family homes. According to tradition, it was commissioned by a Mrs. Pratt after she admired Morris's likeness of a relative. The artist worked on the portrait of her children in several sessions, but when he arrived for the final sitting he was drunk. His patron was torn between her desire to have the portrait finished and her concern for her children's safety. She decided to let the artist proceed, and was relieved that the finished rendering was a good likeness.

This is apparently the portrait of three children that Clara Endicott Sears described in *Some American Primitives*.[3] Sears related virtually the same anecdote, identifying the artist as Morris. Family genealogical notes suggest that this portrait depicts three of the five children born between 1829 and 1836 to John Ball Pratt, Lt. Joel Pratt's son, and his wife Elizabeth Wheelock.[4]

[1] Morris Family Research File, Sterling Historical Society (SHS).
[2] Portrait of Lt. Joel Pratt, SHS.
[3] Clara Endicott Sears, *Some American Primitives: A Study of New England Faces and Folk Portraits* (Boston: Houghton Mifflin Co., 1941), 59-60.
[4] Pratt Family Research File, SHS.

67.
ISAAC SAUNDERS (1808-1888)
Sanford Mason (1798-1865)
Saundersville, R.I., 1846
Oil on panel
14 7/16 x 11 7/8 (37 x 30.2)
Inscribed verso: *S. Mason pinxt,/ July 1846/ 42 years old the next November*
Old Sturbridge Village

SANFORD MASON'S MAGISTERIAL depiction of Isaac Saunders sets the industrialist against a view of his cotton mill. Of the more than thirty known portraits by Sanford Mason, this is the only one with such a detailed background.[1] Saundersville Mill is shown as a white clapboard building with a cupola and

Cat. 67

a full clerestory monitor roof. This feature, a roof raised by a single row of window lights to make the attic space usable, was common in New England textile mills and gave them a distinctive form. As American cotton production increased in importance, the image of the mill came to symbolize New England's industrial might.[2] Here it also signifies the seat of Isaac Saunders's power and the source of his wealth.

Not visible in the portrait is the mill village of Saundersville that grew up around the cotton manufactory. That manufacturing community, like hundreds dotting the New England landscape by the 1830s, encompassed dwellings, a store, and possibly a church or a school for the mill workers and their families. Such villages, or "little hamlets...gathered around the waterfall that serves to turn the mill wheel,"[3] usually developed on the outskirts of an established country town. Saundersville was part of Scituate, a town that, with three rivers to provide water power, was ripe for industrial development. When Isaac Saunders built his mill in 1834, there were already six other mill villages within the town. By

1846, when he sat for his portrait, that number had doubled.[4]

Rhode Island was at the center of the American cotton industry, beginning with the historic establishment in 1793 of Samuel Slater's Pawtucket mill. By the time Saunders founded his manufactory, there were more than one hundred cotton mills in Rhode Island employing some 8,500 people.[5] Saunders entered this industry with financial assistance from his uncle, Thomas Harkness.[6] The partners built the "Upper Mill" on the banks of the Moswaniscut River and were producing cotton cloth by 1835.[7]

Saunders was among the manufacturers who weathered the financial panic of 1837 and prospered with the region's textile industry in the mid-1840s.[8] His choice in 1846 to commission a portrait celebrating his success, linking it to his mill, suggests that his business was securely established. However, the mill did not fare as well in the aftermath of the depression of 1857, and Saunders retired from manufacturing.[9]

Saunders's portrait-sitting also coincided with his 1846 election to the Rhode Island House of Representatives. During the two decades of his business's growth, Saunders became increasingly involved in local and state politics. Like most men who were prominent in their communities, he held a number of town offices, including justice of the peace and town meeting moderator. His career in state government culminated with his election as lieutenant governor in 1859, after which he retired from public office until his re-election to the legislature for three terms in the 1870s.[10] In the interim, Saunders served as president of the Citizens Union Bank.[11]

Isaac Saunders's likeness was captured at a consummate moment of his life in business and politics. At the midpoint of the second and longest of his three marriages, seven of his ten children had been born.[12] By contrast, when Sanford Mason visited Saundersville, the forty-eight year old artist's career had stalled.

Mason began his work as a portraitist at least thirty years earlier, for in 1816 he took the likeness of a man from the Vinton family of Providence, R.I., the painter's birthplace.[13] Like most non-academic artists, Mason emerged from the tradition of ornamental painting, advertising himself as "a portrait and sign painter," who executed "Plain, Ornamental, Sign, Fancy and Chair Painting, and Gilding."[14] Early in his career his travels were confined to Providence and Philadelphia.

It was in the latter city that he met Henrietta Hailer Brasson, whom he married in 1821.[15] The couple's first child, Ann Eliza, was born in Philadelphia before they returned to Providence, where a son, William Sanford, was born in 1824.[16]

After his marriage, Mason re-established Rhode Island as his base, living first in Providence and later in Newport. He gained some public visibility, exhibiting at the Boston Athenaeum Gallery in 1827 and 1828 and at the Pennsylvania Academy of Fine Arts in 1831.[17] By 1830 he and his growing family had a permanent residence in Newport,[18] from which he traveled to Hartford, Boston, New Bedford, Lowell, and Nantucket in search of commissions.

During the 1840s Mason again divided his time between Providence and Philadelphia, where his eldest son William was working as a painter. In 1846, when Isaac Saunders was painted, Mason had a studio in Providence, where he sold copies of portraits, such as his painting of Benjamin Franklin after Edward Savage's 1793 mezzotint.[19] Saunders may have visited the studio to commission his portrait or perhaps Saundersville attracted the artist, as the much larger manufacturing town of Lowell had in the 1830s (see cat. 68). By 1850, Mason was alternating two-year residences in Boston and Philadelphia, relying on his brother and his son for lodging. This atypical pattern continued until his death in Philadelphia in 1865 and is suggestive of the artist's inability to establish a secure and stable situation in his later life.

[1] Information courtesy of the research files of John Obed Curtis. The companion portraits to this painting (coll. Old Sturbridge Village) show Saunders' wife, Maritta Salisbury, and sister, Mary, seated by windows looking onto stylized landscapes.
[2] Richard M. Candee, "The Early New England Textile Village in Art," *Antiques*, 94 (December 1970): 910-911.
[3] Zachariah Allen, *Science of mechanics, as applied to the present improvements in the useful arts in Europe and in the United States of America* (Providence: Hutchins & Cory, 1829). See also, *The New England Mill Village, 1790-1860*, eds. Gary Kulik, Roger Parks, and Theodore Z. Penn (Cambridge, Mass.: The MIT Press, 1982).
[4] Old Sturbridge Village Mill Village Survey, 1969-1972, OSV Research Library.
[5] Joseph Brennan, *Social Conditions in Industrial Rhode Island* (Washington, DC: The Catholic University of America, 1940), 25.
[6] *History of Providence County, R.I.*, ed. Richard M. Bayles, II (New York: W.W. Preston & Co., 1891), 606.
[7] The mill burnt in 1895—the area where it stood is now submerged beneath the Scituate Reservoir.
[8] Brennan, *Industrial Rhode Island*, 29.
[9] Hedley Smith, *The History of Scituate, R.I.* (Scituate, RI: Bicentennial Committee, 1976), 143.

[10] Saunders served in the House of Representatives in 1846, 1847, 1849, 1857, 1858, 1871, and he was elected to the State Senate in 1855, 1872, and 1873; C.C. Beaman, *An Historical Sketch of Scituate, R.I.* (Phenix: Capron & Campbell, 1877), 4; Bayles, *History of Providence*, 621-622.

[11] Bayles, *History of Providence*, 622.

[12] Saunders married: Mary Ann Cushman (1806-1833) in 1830 with whom he had two daughters, Elizabeth and Mary; Maritta Salisbury (1810-1860) in 1834, who bore him seven children, Esther (1836-1839), Abel (1838-1839), Isaac (1840-1905), Sarah (n.d), Infant (1846), Anthony (1850-1875), Clifford (1855-1857); and Ann Eliza Chamberlain (b. 1824) in 1865, who bore one son, Robert H. Saunders (b. 12 August 1865); from Harold A. Vars, "Records of Tobias Saunders and His Descendants" (unpublished typescript, 1971), 156, Westerly Public Library.

[13] Portrait dated September 1816, collection Providence Athenaeum, Providence, R.I.

[14] *Providence Directory* (1824); *Providence Gazette* (1 May 1824).

[15] *Rhode Island American* (23 March 1821).

[16] Ann Eliza Mason died in Providence on 15 November 1822; see, Alverado Hayward Mason, *Genealogy of the Sampson Mason Family* (East Braintree, Mass., 1902).

[17] Information courtesy of the Boston Atheneum and the Philadelphia Academy of Fine Arts.

[18] The 1830 Population Census of Rhode Island lists Sanford Mason heading a household of eight people in Newport; the 1840 Census for Newport lists seven people in the Mason household. Thanks to Maureen Taylor, Reference Librarian, R.I. Historical Society, for providing this information.

[19] John F. Moore, *Providence Almanac and Business Directory* (Providence, 1846), 175.

68.
SARAH SHEDD (1813-1868)
Sanford Mason (1798-1865)
Lowell, Mass., 1833
Oil on canvas
26 x 21 13/16 (66.1 x 55.4)
Inscribed verso: *S. Mason Pinx*/ Lowell 1833
Private collection
Plate 13

THE TEXTILE MANUFACTURING CITIES that drew young women to work in their factories were also magnets for itinerant artists. Portraitists competed for a share of the wages that mill operatives spent on goods and services, ranging from the latest fashions to piano lessons. The "pretty girls in mill & factories some very remarkable beautiful & smart with money plenty," induced Augustus Fuller to set up a studio in Lowell for the first half of 1843.[1] That center of the cotton industry also attracted Sanford Mason for long stretches of time in the 1830s, while Joseph Whiting Stock found ample patronage in New Bedford as well as smaller mill villages such as Cabotville, Mass.[2] Despite

this, portraits of women known to have worked in the factories are extremely rare. The inscription "Lowell, 1833" on the reverse of this painting, places Sarah Shedd's portrait sitting in the city where she worked dressing looms for over a decade.[3]

Cat. 68

After her father died, Shedd went to work to support her family. She began to teach school in her home town of Washington, N.H. in 1828 and soon after established a pattern of teaching in the summer and working as a mill operative in the winter.[4] She paid for her brother's education, and when he and her older sister moved to the West, Shedd assumed full responsibility for her mother. In 1833, her youngest sister died of consumption.[5] The history of this portrait is that she commissioned it after her sister's death as a memento for her mother. It was deemed a successful likeness:

> Her personal appearance was no more ordinary than her mind. Her portrait gives one a good idea of her face, except that her hair was very dark. She had neither regular features or a fine complexion, but her face was very winning. She was above the medium highth and always and everywhere had an inborn dignity, grace, and self-possession.[6]

After 1840 Shedd was primarily employed in the mills—at Lowell until at least 1845 and then in Biddeford, Me.; Salem, Mass.; and Lancaster, Penn. She found peers there who shared her interests in music, poetry, ethics, and philosophy. In 1847 a co-worker described her as "so good so gentle so ladylike & so very fond of her books; she understands five languages & thinks of beginning German."[7]

A writer of poetry and prose, Shedd contributed to *The Lowell Offering*, a journal published by mill girls. Following her death, her poetry was published in a small volume. Mostly she wrote of nature and nostalgia for her childhood home. As she explained:

> Wonder not, then, that pent up within the brick walls of a city I look back with such devotion to the green fields, and gentle streams, to the hills and mountains & forests, to the pure breezes and starry skies of my country home.[8]

Following her mother's death in 1860, Shedd began

Cat. 69

to save money to found a public library. She bequeathed her entire estate of $2500 to the town of Washington for that purpose.[9] In 1869, two years after her death, the townspeople opened the lending library in borrowed rooms, and in 1881 the Shedd Free Library's collection was moved to a new building. That building still stands as a monument to Sarah Shedd's generosity and love of learning.

[1] Augustus Fuller to Aaron Fuller, 24 January 1843, Fuller/Negus Papers.
[2] Groce and Wallace, *Dictionary of Artists in America*, 428, 605; *The Journal of J.W. Stock*, ed. Tomlinson.
[3] "Introduction," *Poems of Sarah Shedd, Founder of the Shedd Free Library* (Washington, NH, 1883), v.
[4] Sarah Shedd, "My Experience as a Teacher," *The Lowell Offering* (November 1845), 260-2.
[5] *History of Washington, N.H., from the First Settlement to the Present Time, 1768-1886* (Claremont, N.H.: Claremont Manufacturing Co., 1886), 260-1, 605.
[6] *Poems of Sarah Shedd*, vi.
[7] Eliza Adams to Hannah Adams, 27 May 1847, private collection.
[8] Sarah Shedd, "My Country Home," 30 March 1847, Lancaster, Penn., autograph album of Eliza Adams, private collection.
[9] *Poems of Sarah Shedd*, v.; Will of Sarah Shedd, 15 March 1867, transcription provided by Sally Krone, Town Historian, Washington, N.H.

69.
HARRIET EDSON SKERRY (1802-1851)
Unknown artist
Oakham, Mass., c. 1828-1832
Oil on canvas
26 3/8 x 23 1/2 (70.1 x 59.7)
Estate of William H. Short

70.
EBENEZER WARD SKERRY (1801-1838)
Unknown Artist
Oakham, Mass., c. 1828-1832
Oil on canvas
26 3/8 x 23 3/8 (70.1 x 59.4)
Estate of William H. Short

PAINTED WHILE THE SKERRYS were still in their twenties, these portraits show a couple secure in their social and economic position and optimistic about

Left: fig. 21 Harriet Edson Skerry, daguerreotype, c. 1845-51. Estate of William H. Short; photographs by Clem Fiori.

their future. They already had several young children, and Ebenezer Skerry was establishing himself as a local businessman. He was postmaster of Oakham, as indicated by the letter held by his wife, and he was an innkeeper and a shareholder in a store,[1] the ledgers of which are proudly displayed behind him.

By 1835, Skerry had moved his family to Hadley, Mass., where he continued to invest in business ventures and real estate. In the fall of 1837, already heavily invested in land and buildings, he mortgaged his house and part of his business to finance a new store. When he died in February, 1838, intestate, he left Harriet with debts of $8,000 and the care of six children under the age of eight. New England was in the midst of a financial panic, and when his real estate, valued at $3,445, was sold at public auction it realized less than half that amount.[2]

Harriet Skerry and her children were left homeless, with only a portion of the household goods valued at $275.25. Among the possessions she retained were a luster tea set, a looking glass, and this pair of portraits. The rest of the household furniture was sold at auction, including beds and bedding, sets of chairs, tables, bureaus, a cook stove, kettles, and other cooking utensils.[3]

In the fourteen years of her widowhood, Harriet's life was one of sustained hardship. She was separated from her children, both by economic necessity and by death. Immediately following her husband's death, her two eldest sons were sent to live with their grandparents, where they attended school and worked binding shoe uppers. The need for her children, not yet legally of age, to earn money speaks of Harriet's impoverishment. Her suffering was intensified by the deaths of two of her children in 1839 and 1841. Her grief was palpable when she wrote to her sons of the death of their sister:

> she has left us, never to return & [I] feel it terribly...although she had seen but a little more than three years, yet she had experienced much pain and suffering and now I trust that she is not only free from sin and sorrow, but is happy in the bosom of her Saviour.[4]

Lacking property and any means of support, Harriet Skerry was forced to rely on her parents and siblings, living as a subordinate member of their households. At the time of her death in 1851, she and her youngest child were living with her sister and brother-in-law in Somerville, Mass.[5]

[1] H.B. Wright and E.D. Harvey, *The Settlement and Story of Oakham, Mass.*, II (New Haven, 1947), 1069; U.S. Post Office Department, Appointment of Ebenezer Skerry as Postmaster, Oakham, Mass., 1 September 1828 (estate of William H. Short); *Massachusetts Register* (Boston, 1832), 94.
[2] Hampshire County, Mass., Deeds, various transactions, 1835-1837; Ebenezer W. Skerry to Elias Hibbard, 4 November 1837; Death notice, *Hampshire Gazette*, 14 February 1838; Hampshire County, Mass., Probate Records, Northampton, Records of Estate Administration, box 132, file #46.
[3] Widow's Allowance and Probate Inventory, Records of Estate Administration; the portraits, tea set and looking glass descended in the Skerry family.
[4] Wright & Harvey, *Story of Oakham*, II, 1069; Harriet Skerry to William Henry and Edward Skerry, c. 1839, (estate of William H. Short).
[5] Population Schedules, Somerville, Mass., U.S. Census, 1850, 324: 374 (microfilm).

Cat. 70

71.
PERMELIA FOSTER SMITH (1806-1880)
Ezra Woolson (1824-1845)
Mont Vernon, N.H., 1842
Oil on canvas
60 1/2 x 48 1/2 (153.7 x 123.2)
Inscribed verso: *E. Woolson Pinxt May 1842*
Old Sturbridge Village
Plate 20

72.
JESSE KITTREDGE SMITH (1804-1851)
Ezra Woolson (1824-1845)
Mont Vernon, N.H., 1842
Oil on canvas
60 1/2 x 48 1/2 (153.7 x 123.2)
Inscribed verso: *A Portrait of Dr. Smith/ E Woolson Pinxt 1842*
Old Sturbridge Village
Plate 21

Cat. 71

THESE NEARLY LIFE-SIZE, full-length images are a late manifestation of an 18th-century portrait tradition. Very rare by 1842, these large-scale portraits raise interesting questions about the training of Ezra Woolson. They suggest that he had seen works by, or influenced by artists such as Ralph Earl (fig. 6) and John Brewster. The complex composition and anatomical representation made these portraits an ambitious undertaking for an artist of only eighteen. Just three years after Woolson painted them he died suddenly during a visit to Fitzwilliam, N.H.:

> Ezra Woolson in 22nd year of his age. He was here taking likenesses at which he had good encouragement and succeeded well. A fever took him off, and he was carried to Milford, N.H. where he belonged, for inturnment.[1]

Half-length portraits of men and women usually included a single object to define gender roles (see cats. 2, 3), but here Dr. and Mrs. Smith's different arenas are described in fully realized environments. Jesse Smith, a physician, is seated in his office, while the companion portrait shows Permelia in her parlor. Outside the window in each painting is a view of the building in which its sitter is portrayed: Dr. Smith's office is shown in the center of town, with vehicles passing by, and the Smith home is illustrated nestled

Cat. 72

in the countryside.

The 19th-century culture of domesticity that contrasted female responsibilities in the home with male commerce in the world, defined raising children as a woman's chief purpose. Interestingly, Permelia Smith never bore any children, and she is depicted as a woman of leisure. Dressed for receiving visitors, she has been interrupted while reading and leans on a table where her needlework has been set aside. She is not engaged in making garments to clothe her family, but is working on a decorative, lace-edged piece of white work. A specialized sewing box holds her supply of silk threads. The watch tucked into her bodice offers an additional measure of her affluence and alludes to the management of work within her home.

Permelia Smith was assisted in running her home by a servant, Hannah Lamson. When Dr. Smith died in 1851 he left Hannah three hundred dollars in recognition of her dedicated service.[2] The year before his death, the doctor was also employing a male laborer, probably to manage his substantial farm.[3]

Dr. Smith's professional work was centered at his office. The surgical tools, medicines, and tooth-pulling key arrayed beside him show the varied medical services he provided. The inventory of the office that was taken when Smith died suggests that the painting represents it accurately. Listed in the inventory are five chairs, a table and cover, a pharmacopeoia, and surgical instruments. Not shown in this painting are his medical library, a skeleton and case, and the mortar, scale, and weights he used in the preparation of medicines.

[1] Notes of the Reverend John Sabin, Fitzwilliam, N.H., January 1845.
[2] Hillsborough County, N.H., Probate Records, Courthouse, Manchester, Docket #08850, Jesse K. Smith, 1851 (will and inventory).
[3] Population Schedules, Mont Vernon, N.H., U.S. Census, 1850, 434: 141; Jesse K. Smith Inventory.

73.
LAURA NEGUS SPOONER (1805-1851)
Attributed to Caroline Negus (1814-1867)
Petersham, Mass., c. 1833
Watercolor on ivory
4 x 3.5 (10.2 x 8.9)
Petersham Historical Society, Inc., Petersham, Mass.

THIS MINIATURE PORTRAIT has long been at-

Cat. 73

tributed to the subject's brother, Nathan Negus (cat. 59). Yet the details of Laura Negus Spooner's appearance, including the gathered bodice and full sleeves of her dress, her sheer ruffled collar, and her hairstyle, indicate a date of the early 1830s, almost ten years after Nathan's death. It is far more likely that this is an early work by Laura's sister, Caroline, an artist known for her miniature portraits (cat. 74).

Unlike full-sized oil portraits, miniatures offered intimate images that could be carried as mementos or shared among family members. Indeed, the Neguses valued these small portraits as visual records of relatives. When Joseph Negus died in Alabama his sister, Fanny (cat. 33), wrote to Nathan, "we feel it a great privilege to have Joseph's portrait," and asked "I wish verry much to see Joseph widdow; cannot you paint her miniature and send it to us?"[1]

Laura Negus Spooner shared the family passion for preserving the histories of its members. Illness plagued the Negus households and by the time this miniature was painted Laura had lost her father and seven of her fourteen siblings.[2] Perhaps the overwhelming loss of so many beloved family members prompted her to begin keeping a scrapbook. In 1844, when her sister Fanny was bedridden, Laura sent her the scrapbook in the hope that it would "bequite a dull hour," with the warning to "be careful of it & every paper for I prize them all."[3] Not unusual in its compilation and preservation of written memorabilia, the Negus family was fortunate to have members whose artistic skill could preserve their likenesses, as well.

[1] Fanny Negus Fuller to Nathan Negus, 18 April 1824, Fuller/Negus Papers.
[2] The seven Negus children who died before 1830 were: Horace (1791-1792), Pamela (1792-1806), Rosanna (1794-1817), Mehitable (1796-1810), Joseph (1797-1823), Nathan (1801-1825), Mary (1808), V.R., Petersham, Mass.
[3] Laura Negus Spooner to Fanny Fuller, 26 October 1844, Fuller/Negus Papers.

74.

MARY ANGELA NEGUS SPOONER
(1811-1886) AND HER CHILDREN
GEORGE (1833-1876) AND CAROLINE
(1835-1856)
Caroline Negus (1814-1867)
Petersham, Mass., c. 1835
Watercolor and crayon on cardboard (marked: *Extra London Board/ De La Rue, Cornish & Rock*)
Inscribed verso: *Painted by/ Aunt Caroline Negus Hildreth / some of her first work / great grandma Angela Spooner/ grandfather George H. Spooner/ Caroline Negus Spooner.*
6 3/8 x 8 9/16 (16.2 x 21.7)
Old Sturbridge Village

ARTISTIC ABILITY RAN in the Negus family, and three of Joel and Basmeth's fourteen children, Joseph, Nathan (cat. 59), and Caroline, used their skill at drawing and painting to support themselves. Mary Angela was known for her artistic nature as expressed in her love of flowers, pictures, and needlework.[1] The prominent bouquet of flowers in this portrait attests to this recollection, while the skillful rendering reveals her sister Caroline's talents.

Mary Angela and Caroline, the two youngest Negus children, were only five and two when their father (cat. 58) died in 1816 at the age of forty-nine, precipitating

the permanent disruption of his household. Only Mary Angela and Caroline continued to live with their mother, while their older siblings boarded with relatives or left Petersham to find work. When Basmeth Negus gave up keeping house in 1823, her youngest daughters followed their siblings out into the world. Lacking the security of a parental household, the Negus children became very independent and had a wide range of experiences.

Initially, Mary Angela found a home in Deerfield with her sister Fanny (cat. 33) and Fanny's husband, Aaron Fuller. She attended Deerfield Academy, where the "fundamental branches of Education" were taught, as well as the ornamental arts.[2] A watercolor painting attributed to Mary Angela, depicting a romantic landscape with a castle, shows her mastery of the decorative artwork taught at female academies.[3] In the spring of 1824, Caroline joined her sisters in Deerfield, where she, too, attended school, possibly at the academy.[4] In the early 1830s, she attended Catherine Fisk's Female Seminary in Keene, N.H., which also emphasized the ornamental arts.[5]

Caroline's artistic skills were nurtured at the schools she attended, as well as by her family. Although her father and two brothers were painters, she probably learned from their example and not from their tutelage, for all had died or left home by the time she was three. The family's artistic talents extended beyond Caroline's siblings—her sister's stepson Augustus Fuller was also an artist. Augustus was only two years older than Caroline, and they formed a friendship, founded on their artistic ambitions, that lasted throughout their lives.[6] Both Augustus and Caroline received their only formal training during brief periods of study with the artist Chester Harding.[7]

Caroline Negus established herself as an artist in Boston. This early picture contains all the hallmarks of her later work. Watercolor and crayon were her preferred media, and the fine detail in the faces shows her ease with working in a miniaturized format. The almost photographic accuracy of the faces contrasts sharply with the coarse execution of the setting, suggesting that she rarely painted genre scenes like this one. Throughout her adult life she worked independently as an artist, building a reputation for her skill as a painter of miniature portraits. Even after her marriage in the mid-1840s to the historian Richard Hildreth, Caroline continued to pursue her vocation,

first in Boston and later in New York and Europe.[8]

Unlike her sister, Mary Angela remained an amateur artist, dedicating her adult life to her family and their home. Caroline may have painted the scene to commemorate the birth of her namesake, Mary Angela's second child, Caroline Negus Spooner. Her intimate representation of the family group captures the loving relationship of a mother and her children. A year or two after this picture was painted Mary Angela nearly died giving birth to her third child. While recuperating at the home of her sister, Laura (cat. 73), her husband, Stevens Spooner, took care of young Caroline while George stayed with his aunt Fanny. Letters written during Mary Angela's recovery offer a glimpse of the affectionate family bond:

> I think much of my dear little George tell him that his mother is so much better that she does not lay on the bed all the time now that his father wants to see his soldier very much, speaks of him often, and Carry says every hour in the day

almost "where's George."[9]

This painting offers contemporary viewers a look into the tender relations of a 19th-century family and survives as an important document of Caroline Negus's early work.

Cat. 74

[1] Negus family genealogy, typescript, Petersham Historical Society, Petersham, Mass.
[2] Deerfield Academy Trustees' Minute Book, December 1825, quoted in Suzanne L. Flynt, *Ornamental and Useful Accomplishments: Schoolgirl Education and Deerfield Academy 1800-1830* (Deerfield, MA: Pocumtuck Valley Memorial Association and Deerfield Academy, 1988), 47.
[3] "The Castle" is illustrated in Flynt, *Ornamental and Useful Accomplishments*, 47.
[4] Aaron Fuller to Nathan Negus, 18 April 1824, Fuller/Negus Papers.
[5] Catherine Fisk to Aaron Fuller, 5 April 1833, Fuller-Higginson Papers, Box 1, Folder 4; Fanny Fuller to Aaron Fuller, 31 May c. 1833, Fuller/ Negus Papers.
[6] Augustus Fuller correspondence, Fuller/Negus Papers.
[7] Receipt from Chester Harding to Aaron Fuller, 12 May 1833, Fuller/ Negus Papers; Howe, *Sketches of Petersham*, 41.
[8] Groce and Wallace, *Dictionary of Artists in America*, 467; Sheldon, *History of Deerfield*, II: 200-1.
[9] Mary Angela Spooner to Fanny Fuller, c. 1837, Fuller/Negus Papers.

75.
DELIA WILLIAMS ELLSWORTH
TAINTOR (1818-1889)
Charles Bird King (1785-1862)
Washington, D.C., c. 1840-1841
Oil on canvas
30 x 25 (76.2 x 63.5)
Private Collection

76.
HENRY GRISWOLD TAINTOR
(1813-1889)
Charles Bird King (1785-1862)
Washington, D.C., c. 1840-1841
Oil on canvas
30 x 25 (76.2 x 63.5)
Private Collection

DURING THEIR 1840 visit to Washington, D.C., Henry and Delia Taintor went to the gallery and studio of Charles Bird King to sit for these portraits.

Cat. 75

They paid the artist one hundred dollars for his work[1]—as much as ten times the price the couple might have paid had they patronized an itinerant artist in Hampton, Conn., their home. Unlike "the mass of folks," who could not "judge of the merits of a well finished picture,"[2] this couple's taste for art in the academic tradition led them to patronize an artist trained in England, whose prices reflected his elite status. The informality and directness of these paintings are characteristic of King's presentation of portrait subjects.[3] Among the elements that distinguish his style from a limner's are the use of intense shading and a varied palette.

The Taintors were newly married when they traveled to Washington to visit Delia's sister.[4] Henry, a merchant farmer like his father, had met Delia, a member of the prominent Ellsworth family, through relatives in Hartford. It was probably she who influenced the decision to commission these portraits. The granddaughter of Oliver Ellsworth, third chief justice of the United States, Delia had always known the monumental Ralph Earl portrait of her grandparents (fig.6), which hung in the drawing room of "Elmwood," the family home in Windsor, Conn.[5] This childhood exposure to a sophisticated painting style must have shaped her aesthetic sensibility and her understanding of portraits as emblems of social position.

The aspiration implicit in Henry and Delia's patronage of King is also evident in their ambitious updating of the Taintor homestead in Hampton. Although the house had been improved when the Taintor family bought it in 1804, the newlyweds modernized and enlarged the structure.[6] Again, Delia had as a model her grandfather and his creation in "Elmwood" of a family homestead and symbol.[7] All five of the Taintors's children were born in the refurbished house, and the couple resided there until their deaths in 1889, just before their fiftieth wedding anniversary. An 1890 inventory of the building's contents places Delia and Henry's portraits in the south front room, along with a photograph of the double portrait of Oliver and Abigail Ellsworth.[8]

The studio where these portraits were painted was a far cry from the rustic surroundings in which Charles Bird King had worked during his years as a traveling painter. A visitor to King's gallery claimed that it afforded "the amateur and admirer of the arts one of the most agreeable lounges in Washington," with walls hung with "fine paintings, consisting of portraits, landscapes, fancy pieces, &c." There the Taintors may have viewed King's genre scene "The Itinerant Artist" (plate 11) in which he recalled the circumstances of his early career, for that painting was deemed among "the most beautiful" in his gallery.[9]

Like many of his contemporaries, King had used his period of itinerancy to establish himself as an independent artist. However, unlike most of his peers, when he began his travels he already had extensive training in the fine arts. Sizable inheritances assured King's financial independence and enabled the native of Newport, R.I. to study art, first in New York City and then in England. His studies at the Royal Academy began in 1806 and continued until the outbreak of the War of 1812 forced him to return to the United States. While in London his instructors were such masters as Benjamin West and Henry Fuseli and among his classmates were Washington Allston, Samuel Morse, Thomas Sully, and John Trumbull. Upon returning to America, King had difficulty finding a similar artistic community or attracting attention to his work. Consequently, he spent the years between 1812 and 1819 traveling, spending time in Newport, Philadelphia, Baltimore, and Richmond, and repeatedly visiting Washington.[10]

A turning point in King's career came in 1815 with the first of many commissions he received to paint the likenesses of distinguished Americans for Joseph Delaplaine's portrait gallery. At the end of 1818, Delaplaine sent King to Washington to paint a portrait of John Quincy Adams.[11] The artist was so well received that he settled in the capital, taking likenesses of men of state and executing his famous series of portraits of native Americans. While King disdained the American taste for portraits above all other forms of painting, he ultimately capitalized on that taste, using it to finance his gallery and his work in other genres.

[1] A receipt in the collection of the owner reads: "Washington March 6th 1841/ Received of H. G. Taintor/ One Hundred Dollars in full/ for the portrait of himself/ and Lady Charles B. King."
[2] John Vanderlyn to John Vanderlyn Jr., 9 September 1825, quoted in Jaffee, "'One of the Primitive Sort'," 103.
[3] See Andrew F. Cosentino, *The Paintings of Charles Bird King, 1765-1862* (Washington: Smithsonian Institution Press, 1977).
[4] Henry Griswold Taintor and Delia Williams Ellsworth were married by the Reverend Spofford D. Jewett in Windsor, Conn. on 25 September 1839.
[5] For additional information about the Earl portrait of Oliver and

Abigail Ellsworth see *The Great River, Art & Society in the Connecticut Valley, 1635-1820* (Hartford, CT: Wadsworth Atheneum, 1985), 155.
[6] The business and personal papers of Henry and Delia Taintor are in a private collection.
[7] Alberta Eiseman, "20th-Century Technology Preserves A Rare Sample of 18th-Century Life," *The New York Times*, 29 September 1991, sec. 12:2.
[8] Inventory taken by Mary Taintor Davis, private collection.
[9] George Watterston, *A New Guide to Washington* (Washington, R. Farnham; New York, S. Colman, 1842) 102.
[10] Cosentino, *Paintings of C.B. King*, 11-26.
[11] Ibid.

Cat. 76

77.
LOIS ANN THAYER (1821-?)
Augustus Fuller (1812-1873)
Springfield, Mass., c. 1839-1844
Watercolor on Ivory
2 3/16 x 1 3/4 (5.55 x 4.5)
Inscribed verso: *Augustus Fuller / Deaf & Dum[b]/ Artis[t]/ $30. 18*
Pocumtuck Valley Memorial Association, Memorial Hall Museum, Deerfield, Mass.

MINIATURES ENJOYED GREAT POPULARITY in the first half of the 19th century. Unlike the more

Cat. 77; photograph by Chuck Kidd

to New Haven, Conn. Her bare head and shoulders suggest a woman in her late teens or early twenties who had not yet assumed the symbolic garb of cap and collar worn by married women.

[1] Account by George Fuller of Augustus Fuller's portraits & miniatures painted in New York in 1840 and 1841, Fuller-Higginson Papers, Box 14, Folder 3.
[2] Ibid.: see also Augustus Fuller Correspondence, Fuller/Negus Papers.
[3] Augustus Fuller to Aaron Fuller, 19 August 1840, Fuller/Negus Papers.

78.
DOLLY FLOYD WILEY (1811-1884)
Erastus Salisbury Field (1805-1900)
Plumtrees (Sunderland), Mass., 1837
Oil on canvas
35 x 29 (88.9 x 73.6)
Museum of Fine Arts, Springfield, Mass.,
The Morgan Wesson Memorial Collection
Plate 5

IN 1837, AFTER A LONG VISIT to the Berkshires (see cats. 12-15, 29), Erastus Salisbury Field returned to his home in Plumtrees (Sunderland), on the Connecticut River in western Massachusetts. He spent most of that year there, busied with painting portraits of friends and relatives. His cousin, Dolly Wiley, sat for the artist, as did her mother, Catherine Dunn Wiley.[1] Mrs. Wiley was depicted in mourning, reflecting a life that had seen the deaths of many loved ones—six of her children had died in August 1803 in a dysentery epidemic and she had lost her husband in 1825.[2] In 1837, Dolly, who never married, was living with her mother in the family home then owned by her brothers John and Ebenezer.

Just as portraits were part of the consumer culture of the 1830s, so too were the stylish dress made of imported silk and the accordion shown in this painting. Through these objects, Wiley linked herself with the class of women who had the leisure time and disposable income to partake of the wide range of domestic and imported goods newly available in rural New England. The red upholstered mahogany chair on which she sits may also be an example of these goods. However, many of Field's subjects are shown sitting in a similar red backed chair (see cats. 14, 15), a form not readily associated with New England. This may have been an idealized chair or a piece owned by

public role of oil portraits in celebrating personal accomplishment, miniatures were keepsakes to be treasured. These personal mementos were often carried by their owners or even worn, such as the pin and locket-sized miniatures that Augustus Fuller made in 1840.[1]

Miniature painting comprised two-fifths of Fuller's business. The thirty-dollar price recorded on the back of this small portrait is surprisingly high for his work and may indicate that it was one of a group. The artist's accounts show that his miniatures commanded an average of five dollars, within a range of three to ten dollars.[2] His most expensive miniature was $15.50,[3] a price influenced by its gold frame, for the value of the other materials was minimal: watercolors were relatively inexpensive, and ivories cost about twenty-five cents apiece.

Fuller frequently passed through Lois Ann Thayer's home town, Springfield, Mass., and his letters describe stays in that city in 1839 and 1842. Lois Thayer probably sat for the artist on one of those visits, before she married Elisha Bliss in 1844 and moved with him the artist; its silhouette suggests a "Voltaire" chair, a New York fashion that Field may have encountered when he was a student in that city.[3]

The diatonic, or ten-keyed, accordion that Wiley holds had been popularized in France less than a decade before this picture was painted. Musical instruments were traditionally symbols of a woman's education and refinement, but in this instance the accordion also demonstrates Wiley's participation in the latest musical fad sweeping New England. Her contemporary, Lucy Goodale, wrote home in the late 1830s that "there are 2 or 3 accordions here and they sound so sweetly that it makes me hope you will take good care of our poor thing."[4] Around the same time, the antislavery activist, Lydia Maria Child, then living in Northampton, Mass., wrote that her husband had "to strike up his accordion to drown" out the racist expressions of a neighbor.[5]

This representation relates to a broader tradition of portraits of single women. At an earlier time, affluent male guardians had commissioned portraits to promote the accomplishments and marriageability of their female charges. In the second quarter of the 19th century, a trend emerged in which single women commissioned their own likenesses to celebrate their autonomy (cats. 1, 2, 68). Either one of these traditions could have motivated the taking of Dolly Wiley's likeness, but ultimately the portrait was a record of the actualities of her life. She never married, nor did she attain financial independence. Rather, she remained a moderately affluent woman who relied on the support of her family and in return provided assistance with the management of the Wiley household.[6]

Cat. 78

[1] Black, *Erastus Salisbury Field*, 26, 104.
[2] J. M. Smith, *History of the Town of Sunderland, Mass.* (Greenfield, Mass.: E.A. Hall, 1899), 575.
[3] Joseph T. Butler, *Field Guide to American Antique Furniture* (New York: Henry Holt and Company, 1985), 4.
[4] Lucy Goodale to Warren Goodale, c. 1837, American Antiquarian Society.
[5] Lydia Maria Child to Caroline Weston, 27 July 1838, Anti-slavery Collection, Boston Public Library, Boston, Mass.
[6] Dolly Wiley's father left his homestead to his sons but provided that his daughter could live their as long as she was unmarried. See: Franklin County, Mass., Probate Records, Docket #5373, Ebenezer Wiley

(will); Population Schedules, Sunderland, Mass., U.S. Census, 1850, 320: 389

79.
UNKNOWN WOMAN, POSSIBLY A MEMBER OF THE FULLER FAMILY
Augustus Fuller (1812-1873)
Probably Connecticut River Valley, c. 1832
Oil on wood panel
24 x 18.5 (61 x 47)
Museum of Fine Arts, Springfield, Mass.,
Gift of Miss Elizabeth Fuller

HAVING DESCENDED in the Fuller family, it is very likely that this painting portrays a relative of the artist's. It may have been painted shortly after 1829, when Augustus completed his education and returned for a time to his family home in Deerfield, Mass. Early in his career he primarily painted miniatures (cat. 34) and oil portraits on wood panels. This portrait panel is the same size as others used by Fuller (cat. 45). The painting, while not as accomplished as the artist's later

Cat. 79

work, is similar in style and composition to other likenesses by him, such as his miniature portrait of Lois Thayer (cat. 77), which also depicts a bare-shouldered young woman seated on an upholstered chair.

By 1832 Fuller had begun to work as an itinerant artist, for in April that year he was in Chatham, Conn., where he received commissions for five or more portraits at ten dollars apiece.[1] That summer he joined his father on a trip to Clinton, N.Y., and in the fall he went on alone to New York City to work briefly for the

Cat. 80

lithographers Thayer and Pendleton.[2] By December he had returned to western Massachusetts, where he advertised: "PORTRAIT PAINTING. AUGUSTUS FULLER, although deaf and dumb, asks for a share of public patronage in his profession. Room over Messrs. Fowle & Kirkland [Northampton, Mass.], where some of his portraits may be seen."[3] The artist's busy

life prompted his aunt, Luthera Negus, to write him these encouraging words:

> I am afraid you work hard as you wrote your arms were lame. I love you dearly, have got your portrait hung up in my parlor, which looks as if it would speak. I am happy to look at it often.[4]

[1] Augustus Fuller to Aaron and Fanny Fuller, 11 April 1832, Fuller-Higginson Papers, Box 5, Folder 6.
[2] Augustus Fuller to Aaron Fuller, 29 July 1832, 7 November 1832, Fuller/Negus Papers; Aaron Fuller to Fanny Fuller, 3 September 1832, Fuller-Higginson Papers, Box 5 Folder 2.
[3] *Hampshire Gazette*, 12 December 1832.
[4] Luthera Negus to Augustus Fuller, 5 August 1832, Fuller-Higginson Papers, Box 1, Folder 4.

80.
UNKNOWN WOMAN
Prior-Hamblen School
Portland, Me. or Boston, Mass., c. 1837-1844
Tempera on academy board
15 1/4 x 10 1/2 (38.7 x 26.7)
Old Sturbridge Village

THE WORKING LIVES of William Matthew Prior and the Hamblen family of painters, also from Bath, Me., were linked by Prior's 1828 marriage to Rosamond Clark Hamblen. When the Priors moved to Portland in the early 1830s, they lived with Nathaniel Hamblen before establishing their own residence, at which two other Hamblen brothers, Joseph and Sturtevant, boarded.[1] By 1841, all were living and working at 12 Chambers Street in Boston, and later on Marion Street.[2] The Priors and Hamblens had moved to separate residences in East Boston by 1844.

The Hamblens were ornamental painters, a trade that had a long history in their family;[3] only Sturtevant advertised as a portrait painter. His surviving works, like Prior's, show that the time spent on a painting determined its price. The general classification of "Prior-Hamblen School" has evolved for unsigned works like this because the two artists worked together for a period and their least developed portraits are stylistically so similar. Another relative, George Hartwell, is also associated with this distinctive style of portraiture.[4]

Most Prior-Hamblen likenesses have an elongated vertical format, are fairly small, and are painted in oil or tempera on heavy cardboard. "Without shade or shadow" was Prior's own description for the two-dimensionality characteristic of these works.[5] The artists's quickly rendered, cartoon-like representations lacked the modelling that would have made the images more sophisticated and lifelike. A label that describes their process is adhered to the back of a Prior portrait and reads: "Portraits/ Painted in this Style!/ Done in an hour's sitting/ Price $2.92, including Frame, Glass &c./ Please call at Trenton Street/ E. Boston/ Wm. M. Prior."[6]

The equation of style and quality with price raises interesting questions about the artistic sensibility of Prior's clientele, and more broadly about the patrons of other non-academic artists. The unknown woman's earrings and the black bands securing her hairstyle are almost identical to Lucy Hartshorn's (cat. 43), yet the two women's portraits, probably by the same artist, are dramatically different. The unknown woman's likeness cost a fraction of Mrs. Hartshorn's. Were price and time, however, the only factors that determined her choice? Was one critic's estimation that "the mass of folks can't judge of the merits of a well finished picture" accurate, suggesting that the unknown woman lacked the refinement to want a more accomplished portrait?[7] The tastes and motivations of these subjects can never be truly known. However, the number of plain, direct portraits that survive strongly suggest that the commissioning and ownership of a self-image had greater significance for many people than the prestige that might have come from owning a work of art.

81.
UNKNOWN WOMAN
New England, c.1840-1850
Daguerreotype of an oil portrait
3 1/4 x 2 3/4 (8.3 x 7)
Old Sturbridge Village

82.
UNKNOWN MAN
New England, c.1840-1850
Daguerreotype of an oil portrait
3 1/4 x 2 3/4 (8.3 x 7)
Old Sturbridge Village

THE TEXTURE OF THE CANVAS clearly visible in these daguerreotypes of two oil portraits shows the clarity of detail that astonished 19th-century Americans when the first photographic process was introduced. Although this tremendous accuracy of representation—and the speed and low cost of

Cat. 81

[1] Nina Fletcher Little, "William Matthew Prior," *Primitive Painters in America*, eds. Lipman and Winchester (NY: Dodd Mead & Company, 1950), 82.
[2] Rumford, *American Folk Portraits*, 112.
[3] George Hamblen trained as a painter and glazier in Barnstable, Mass., and moved to Gorham, Me., in 1763. His son, Almery, was also a house and sign painter who, late in life, was associated with his four sons Joseph G., Nathaniel, Eli (d. 1839), and Sturtevant J. See Rumford, *American Folk Portraits*, 112.
[4] Rumford, *American Folk Portraits*, 112.
[5] *Maine Inquirer*, 5 April 1831.
[6] Illustrated in Nina Fletcher Little, *Little by Little* (New York: E.P. Dutton, Inc., 1984), 114.
[7] John Vanderlyn to John Vanderlyn Jr., 9 September 1825, quoted in Jaffee, "'One of the Primitive Sort'," 103.

producing daguerreotypes—ultimately eroded the market for non-academic portraiture, both modes of capturing a likeness co-existed for several decades.

When Louis J. M. Daguerre demonstrated his invention in Paris in 1839, its long-term implications were quickly understood. "From this day painting is dead," exclaimed the artist Paul

Cat. 82
Delaroche, and the English painter J.M.W. Turner prophesied: "This is the end of art. I am glad I have had my day."[1] However, the experiences of two American artists show that a market for photographic portraits took time to evolve. In April 1840, eight months after Daguerre's introduction of the technique, George Fuller attended a demonstration in Boston of the new method by which drawings were "produced by rays of light upon a plate chemically prepared."[2] He quickly resolved to become a daguerrean artist, with the anticipa-

tion that he could take 50 pictures a day, sell them for seven dollars apiece, and realize a profit of five dollars on each. At the end of that year Fuller and his half-brother Augustus, the portrait painter, set out on a six-month trip through New York state. George charged ten dollars for the novel photographs at a time when Augustus was selling full-sized oil portraits for the same price and miniatures for half that amount.[3] Not surprisingly, George could not compete, and in May 1841 he sold his apparatus at a loss of $20, noting that he was glad to get rid of it at that price.[4]

Photographers who priced their wares more realistically enjoyed greater success. These photographs show one aspect of the daguerrean process that quickly captivated the public: the ability to replicate images. Although each daguerreotype was a unique image, it could be re-photographed, duplicating a picture with only a small loss of detail. Additionally, the process miniaturized its subject, making it portable. The subjects of these two portraits appear to have been fairly elderly when they were painted between 1810 and 1825. When the portraits were photographed in the 1840s, it is probable that the couple had died and that the daguerreotypes made copies of their likenesses available to other family members. Many other examples of daguerreotypes of portraits survive, some of which show a parent with the portrait of a deceased child and others that show children with portraits of themselves at an earlier age.[5]

While daguerreotypes perpetuated painted portraits, they were also used to inform them. By the middle of the 19th-century, many non-academic artists used a photograph of their subject as an aid in painting a portrait. For example, the painter Isaac Augustus Wetherby used daguerreotypes to assist in the painting of posthumous portraits. On other occasions daguerreotypes of living people helped the artist shorten the number of portrait sittings. Photographs also enabled the painter to gather images of dispersed family members as the basis for a group portrait.[6]

This overlap of painted and photographic likenesses shows that people soon became accustomed to the new portrait options and that some acquired self-images created in each medium. Despite the grim forebodings of artists, photography did not completely displace painting. Instead, the market for likenesses at various prices was increased, redefining mass portraiture in a new age.

[1] Quoted in Julian Wolff, "Daguerreotypes as Folk Art," *The Clarion*, 11 (Fall 1986): 19.

[2] George Fuller to Aaron Fuller, 11 April 1840, Fuller-Higginson Papers, Box 1, Folder 7.

[3] Augustus Fuller to Aaron Fuller, 7 June 1841, Fuller/Negus Papers; Account by George Fuller of Augustus Fuller's portraits and miniatures painted in New York in 1840 and 1841, Fuller-Higginson Papers, Box 14, Folder 3.

[4] George Fuller to Aaron Fuller, 1 May 1841, Fuller-Higginson Papers, Box 1, Folder 8.

[5] See Wolff, "Daguerreotypes as Folk Art," 18-24.

[6] Ploog, "Account Books of I.A. Wetherby," 78.

ARTISTS AND PAINTINGS
IN THE EXHIBITION

Ainsworth, William Fisk
Frederick Kilner
Harriet Evelith Kilner
Alexander, Francis
Prudence Crandall
Artist Unknown
Hannah & Mary Adams
Francis Carlisle Babbitt
William Balch
Perley Bartlett
Persis Bartlett
Esther Belcher Bird
Elijah Woodward Carpenter
Stephen Fitch
Allen Frizle
Rufus Frizle
Sabra Frizle
Edward Mellen
Mary Perry
Ebenezer Ward Skerry
Harriet Edson Skerry
Unknown Man & Woman
Bascom, Ruth Henshaw
Ruth Henshaw Bascom
Chin-Sung
Edwin Davis
Moses Green
Mrs. Moses Green
Mary Locke

Belknap, Zedekiah
Elijah Dudley
Nathanael Howe
Asa Knight
Susan Miller Knight
Bowdoin, David Waite
James Bowdoin
Tirzah Waite Bowdoin
Bundy, Horace
Franklin W. Goddard
John M. Goddard
Mary B. Goddard
Nathan W. Goddard
Samuel Humphrey
Field, Erastus Salisbury
Almira Dodge Bassett
Bethiah Smith Bassett
Joseph Bassett
Nathaniel Bassett
Elisha Freeman, Jr.
Dolly Floyd Wiley
Fletcher, Aaron Dean
Hiram Ebenezer Adams
Luthera Adams
Mark White Adams
Philena Allbee Adams
George Perry
Hannah Chandler Perry
Solon Perry

Fuller, Augustus
 Edwards Whipple Denny
 Elizabeth Stone Denny
 Fanny Fuller & Sons
 Mercy Bemis Fuller
 Elihu Hoyt
 Lois Ann Thayer
 Unknown Woman
King, Charles Bird
 Delia Ellsworth Taintor
 Henry Taintor
 The Itinerant Artist
Mason, Sanford
 Isaac Saunders
 Sarah Shedd
Morris, Jones Fawson
 Pratt Children
Negus, Caroline
 Laura Negus Spooner
 Mary Angela Negus Spooner
Negus, Nathan
 Joel Negus
 Nathan Negus
 John Robinson

Peckham, Robert
 Timothy, Susan & Pearson Doty
 Newton Simeon Hubbard
 Sarah Puffer Hubbard
Prior, William Matthew
 Jesse Hartshorn
 Lucy A. Hartshorn
 Nancy Lawson
 William Lawson
 Morse Children
 William Matthew Prior
 Unknown Woman
Smith, Royall Brewster
 John Perrin
Stock, Joseph Whiting
 Edward W. Gorham
Webb, H.T.
 Lewis Ford Baldwin
Woolson, Ezra
 Jesse Kittredge Smith
 Permelia Foster Smith

ABOUT THE AUTHORS

DAVID JAFFEE is Assistant Professor in the Department of History, City College of New York

ELIZABETH MANKIN KORNHAUSER is Curator of American Decorative Arts, Wadsworth Atheneum

JACK LARKIN is Chief Historian, Old Sturbridge Village

JESSICA F. NICOLL is Curator of Exhibits, Old Sturbridge Village

CAROLINE F . SLOAT is Director of Publications, Old Sturbridge Village